These Haunted Halls

Inside America's
Most Haunted School

Robin M. Strom-Mackey

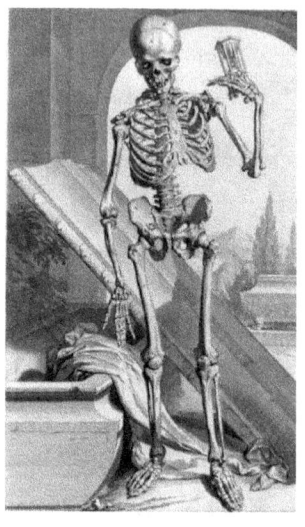

Copyright © 2024 by Robin M. Strom-Mackey

Title: These Haunted Halls - Inside America's Most Haunted School

All rights reserved. No part of this publication may be reproduced, distributed, or transmitted in any form or by any means, including photocopying, recording, or other electronic or mechanical methods, without the prior written permission of the publisher, except in the case of brief quotations embodied in critical reviews and certain other noncommercial uses permitted by copyright law. For permission requests, write to the publisher, addressed "Attention: Permissions Coordinator," at the address below:

White Crow Press

34 N. Erin Avenue

Felton, Delaware 19943

www.delawareparanormalresearchgroup.com

ISBN: 9798218988746

Printed in the United States of America

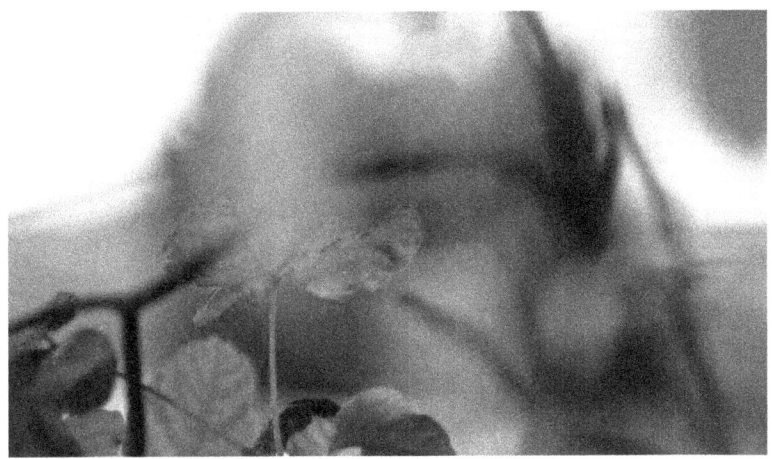

This book is dedicated to Nancy Nutter, my friend, and my confidante. The silence since you've gone is vacuous.

I miss our conversations, I miss your unflagging spirit and courage, even in the face of unsurmountable odds. You rarely gave up hope, even when hope was not viable. If nothing else, you taught me how to have courage, even when courage seems pointless and we seem desperate to fail.

May you rest in peace and not forget our friendship.

Come rattle my cabinets; you know I'd love that. Sometimes I still text…I can't help myself.

I trust you now live in quiet places.

Table of Contents

Preface..7

Chapter One: History of St. Joseph's Industrial School 13

Chapter Two: Providence Creek Academy 61

Chapter Three: Police Get Involved 91

Chapter Four: First State Military Academy 101

Chapter Five: Searching for Proof of a Haunting.................137

Chapter Six: Return to First State 151

Resources 183

Preface

"**M**y People Will Live in Quiet Places"
I must begin at the beginning. I first saw St. Joseph's Industrial School when I was asked to videotape a wedding in the Clayton area some 17 years ago. I drove past the site and stopped. One doesn't expect to see a majestic Catholic Church set behind a decorative arch of brick and wrought iron in the middle of a tiny, rural, Delaware community. There behind the aged iron-work gates, I could see a stately old Chapel that was clearly abandoned. I was struck dumb at the vision. I've had a life-long love of old architecture, and this was a beautiful building. I was so bewildered by the vision that I stopped my car and asked a passerby about the beautiful property. He informed me that it was not being used for anything anymore, although that couldn't have been completely correct. By that time Providence Creek Academy had obtained the buildings and must have been at least restoring the older brick buildings on the property for use by the Charter School.

The Chapel, I would find out later, was Italianate Basilica architecture – very unusual for rural Delaware. Flush with stained glass windows, some 53 of them, it twinkled in the afternoon sunshine. While I'm not a churchgoer by nature, I do have a love of old churches. They hearken back to a time when people would live in a hovel, but give every dime they made to build castles to God. They're edifices of grandeur in an often-unlovely world.

Church with original bell tower

I've never imagined finding God in our new-fangled, WIFI connected world where congregations rent movie theatres, boasting surround sound and big screens. But an old church with the dust motes streaming down from stained-glass windows as a choir sings in perfect harmony amid the smoke of Frankincense slowly wafting in swirling eddies? Therein I think I could find peace.

The Chapel, I would be made to understand, was the centerpiece of what had been a Catholic boarding school, now closed. I asked my new acquaintance about the church. Couldn't they save it, couldn't they do something to restore it? He responded that it would take more money to restore the building than what it was worth. I was appalled. Sometimes humans spend far too much money on crass buildings, while letting architectural monuments decay into obscurity, until they become fodder for the wrecking ball. I asked, certainly it couldn't be left to fall apart? He informed me that it was.

I drove away, saddened that this beautiful property was now empty and desolate. That was my last trip to Clayton for the next fifteen years. As I said before, there is little in rural Clayton but decaying old buildings and the remnants of the old school with its deteriorating Chapel. I learned nothing else about the property. In essence, I forgot about it. It had not forgotten me. Perhaps it was fate.

Step forward 15 years. I was looking at my email one morning when I got a curious message from someone named Janet at First State Military Academy in Clayton, Delaware. "Clayton, Delaware?" I pondered. I'd been to Clayton, and there was nothing there except the moldering old buildings and the abandoned Catholic School. When I started reading the message, I was immediately intrigued. Janet was telling me that First State Military Academy had taken over the old Catholic School, having bought at least some of the property from Providence Creek Academy. Providence Creek Academy I had heard of, having been a high school teacher at another charter school in the area. I had had students that came in, claiming they were from P.C.A. I was amazed. Were we all talking about the same abandoned property I had witnessed 15 years ago?

Janet assured me that the school where she worked was an old property. It had been a Catholic School, then a Charter School, and now was a military school. She had found our site online and wanted us to do a thorough paranormal investigation. If I was interested, she told me I should give her a call. I did so…immediately. One of my team members asked "how did you get so plum an investigation?" I answered, "It was quite unexplainable. They asked out of the blue, and I accepted." These things don't happen every day.

When I arrived, the curious Ms. Janet led me into the front of what is now called Drexel Hall, named for the first lady of the school, the one that funded the establishment, by her sheer generosity, Katherine Drexel.

We went first into the main school office. It was a place where the staff had experienced such phenomena as having unaccountable breezes blow through the room, stirring up papers and knocking pencils off the desk. Janet showed me the infamous C-Wing where actual, full-bodied apparitions had been seen and all manner of strange events occurred. We viewed the equally active A-Wing, which played host to frequent, weird electrical anomalies. Janet informed me that the bathrooms often had water coming on by itself.

We then took a tour of the Chapel and the Chapel's basement, which housed all manner of artifacts from the property's time as St. Joseph's Industrial School. Child sized desks were stacked helter skelter. Boxes of children's textbooks slumped moldering on the damp cement floor; some desks had opened, spilling their contents of old books onto the damp floor. Old Catholic statues of saints and Mother Mary watched us through sightless eyes as we wandered the rows of treasures while the light filtered through grimy windows.

In the Chapel itself only one of the two altars remained, but the Chapel was now barren of pews and sat essentially empty while dust motes danced in the light of the stained-glass windows. In the two rooms off the main altar, we found candelabras now bereft of both candles and purpose. The desks of priests still hid a distant past of old papers, and we found a horde of black and white photographs from the school's days of operation, many of which you will see throughout the book.

That was the start of what would essentially be a three-year obsession for me and the team. We designated a night to do the investigation. The rest, as they say, is history. In this case, a rich and wonderful history.

ROBIN M. STROM-MACKEY

Chapel of St. Joseph's Industrial School

Chapter One:
History of St. Joseph's Industrial School

> "My people will live in a peaceful country.
> In quiet restful places.
> My people will live in quiet places."
> Isaiah 32: 15 *Liturgy of the Hours*

While St. Joseph's Industrial School was initially provided for by the Drexel family, it was run officially by the Josephite Order. A rather obscure order, the Josephites note on their official website that they are a "religious community of Catholic Priests and brothers committed to serving the African American community." The sect derives its name from Joseph, the surrogate father of Jesus, and was chosen to connote the kind and caring fatherly love that Joseph bestowed onto the Son placed under his care. Originally, the Order was concerned with the welfare of both African Americans and Native Americans. They were formed not long after the Civil War and the emancipation of slaves.

The real 'father' of this institution was not Joseph, however, but a priest by the name of Father John A. DeRuyter. DeRuyter organized the St. Joseph Church in Wilmington in 1889, just 24 years after the end of the Civil War. He expanded the role of the Church to include an orphanage, but soon realized that as the boys grew, they needed more opportunities.

"We must have another institution that will make our boys men, that will teach them the dignity of labor and create in them the spirit of industry," wrote DeRuyter. (Taylor)

In just such a spirit of industry, DeRuyter purchased a 200-acre farm in Clayton, Delaware in 1895.

The estate already had a colorful past, having formerly been the estate of the first Delaware governor, Governor Joshua Clayton. Clayton, a medical doctor, first rose to fame when he served as Geroge Washington's personal surgeon during the Revolutionary War.

Father John A. DeRuyter

Joshua Clayton, 1st Governor of Delaware

He would later become the first "President" of Delaware, the title changing to Governor after the state legislators wrote the Delaware Constitution. He served as Governor from January 1 1793 to January 19, 1796. After leaving office he ran and won a seat on the U.S. senate. He died at the age of 54 during the Yellow Fever epidemic at his estate, "Locust Grove (Locust Grove)".

Clayton's former mansion, "Locust Grove" still stood on the property when DeRuyter purchased the old estate. It would become the priests' dormitory, until it burnt to the ground

THE RECTORY   OFFICE AND BROTHERS' RESIDENCE

The other buildings, the buildings for DeRuyter's dream school, would be built by hand. Twenty-five boys, aged 10-17, were sent from the orphanage in Wilmington to Clayton. There they were put to work constructing the buildings that would eventually become the very classrooms and dormitories they would inhabit. Shortly afterwards two additional farms were purchased, and another 200 acres were added. The campus and its fully functioning farm were now 400 acres large.

The school would teach not only reading, writing and arithmetic, but also provide the boys with a trade, whether that be farming or carpentry. Over the course of the next 82 years, the trades the boys were offered would change with the times and the skills the brothers possessed, but these would come to include printing, shoe repair, tailoring, house painting, general farm work, dairy and poultry farming, baking, and domestic science. For the original 25 boys one wonders how many ended up being expert carpenters, having learned the trade in the trenches.

Tragically, Father DeRuyter never saw his dream completed. In August of 1896, just a year into the project, he was at the railroad station in Wilmington, Delaware returning to Clayton when he had a sudden and massive heart attack. He died at the age of 42.

He did return to his beloved school; however, he was buried next to the Chapel. In 1926, his body was disinterred and moved to the school's small graveyard on the back of the property. There his remains rest with several others of his brethren, both Priests,

Brothers, and a few Lay Persons. While tragic, his death did not stop the forward momentum of the school. Building continued.

As noted earlier, the funding for the school came from the Drexel family, in particular Katherine and her sister Louise Drexel Morrell. Katherine Drexel, born November 26, 1858 in Philadelphia, was the daughter of Francis Drexel, and niece to the wealthy Anthony J. Drexel, who established Drexel University in Philadelphia. Francis A. Drexel was the third generation of the Drexel empire started by his grandfather, a banking empire that financed and shaped the economic development of the fledgling United States from the Mexican-American War through the California Gold Rush, the Civil War and into the industrial revolution of the late 19th century. The Drexel family was one of the wealthiest families in America, and their family connections included many of the richest and most powerful among the elites, including former first-lady Jacqueline Kennedy Onassis. Katherine's great grandfather would partner with J.P. Morgan, founding Drexel, Morgan & Co., later renamed simply J.P. Morgan

Francis married Hannah Langstroth in 1854, and the union resulted in two daughters, Elizabeth, and Katherine. Tragically Hannah Langstroth Drexel died three weeks after giving birth to Katherine in 1858. Francis entrusted his brother Anthony and his wife Ellen to raise the two girls until Francis remarried in 1860. His second wife, Emma Bouvier, would eventually give Francis a third daughter, Louise Bouvier Drexel Morrell, born in 1860.

Drexel daughters: Elizabeth Drexel, Louise Bouvier Drexel (Morrell), Katherine Drexel

The girls grew up in a wealthy but highly religious household and were weaned on philanthropic gestures. Francis donated to local hospitals, asylums, orphanages, and other institutions dedicated to assisting the poor and misfortunate. Emma opened their 90-acre estate three times a week, giving out food and clothing. The family donated eleven million dollars a year to the charities of their choosing. While wealth and privilege were bred into Katherine's childhood, they were balanced against charity and service. Her father, Francis, was said to spend much time in prayer daily.

Their step mother, Emma, died in 1883 after a long and contracted battle with cancer, and Katherine marked this as a pivotal point in her life, having nursed her step-mother for three years. In 1884, Katherine traveled with her father and sisters to the western states where she witnessed the destitution of Native

Americans forced to live in poverty, restricted to reservations. It left a lasting impression on the young woman.

In 1885, only a year after his wife passed, Francis died as well. In his will he left ten percent of his earnings to charity. The rest of the fifteen million dollars he possessed passed to the three daughters. Katherine, 27 at that time, became a very wealthy woman overnight. It appears that none of the three daughters ever produced heirs, and when Katherine Drexel died in 1955 as the last heir, the remaining fourteen million dollars was donated to the original charities Francis Drexel had named in his will.

The 27-year-old Katherine, unmarried, and with millions of dollars at her disposal, must have had a moment of reckoning. Philadelphia high society assumed Katherine would do a world tour, become a debutante, and eventually marry and produce Drexel heirs. Katherine, despite her banking empire history, possessed deep religious leanings, and a strong desire to do good works. Even still, I doubt even she had an inkling as to how her life would change.

In 1887, while in Rome, she was allowed a private audience with Pope Leo XIII. She implored him as to the need of nuns to staff mission schools in the U.S., both for the Native American impoverished population and the newly emancipated African-American population. The Pope agreed, under one condition. Katherine was to devote her life, and her vast inheritance…to the Catholic Church. As stunning as this stipulation was, young Katherine took some time to consider the stipulation, but finally conceded.

In 1889, Katherine Drexel, millionaire heiress of a banking empire, became a novice with the Sisters of Mercy in Pittsburgh, Pennsylvania. Two years later, she took her final vows and with a few, fellow sisters founded the Blessed Sacrament Sisters for Indians and Colored People.

Mother Superior, Katherine Drexel

She was named the Superior General. The new community of Sisters moved from the Drexel summer home in Torres Dale, Pennsylvania to the St. Elizabeth's convent in Cornwell Heights, Pennsylvania the following year. They received final papal approval in May of 1913.

In two year's time, the novice became a Mother Superior and her active contributions could begin. And they did, in earnest. She started with the founding of St. Catherine's Boarding School for Pueblo Indians in Santa Fey, New Mexico in 1894. Following closely on the heels, in 1899, she opened a school for African-American girls at Rock Castle, Virginia. In 1903 she financed schools in Arizona and Tennessee. In 1915 she funded perhaps her most provocative endeavor, the opening of a college that would receive the name of Xavier University of Louisiana, the only private, predominantly African American, Catholic university in the United States. She did so in order to have a university to train the educators that would be on the front line in her schools and missions. Today, XULA is the top university in the nation for producing African American doctors.

Mother Katherine was also busily establishing 51 convents. By 1927 she had established convents at Columbus, Ohio, Chicago, Boston, and New York City.

Throughout her tenure, Mother Superior Katherine Drexel established 12 schools for Native Americans, 50 schools for African Americans and 145 missions. Aside from education, the schools offered religious instruction and vocational training. Segregationists and bigots harassed her vehemently, especially in the South where segregation efforts were the most stringent.

Katherine's efforts were met with resistance and often attempts to shut down construction before they opened the doors. When those non-violent injunctions failed, sometimes her enemies threatened violence.

The Order's Mother House in Bensalem, Pennsylvania received a bomb threat when it was under construction. A school in Rock Castle, Virginia was burnt to the ground by arsonists in 1899. The Ku Klux Klan threatened to do the same to a school in Texas. Katherine became adept at hiding her property purchases with dummy corporations and subterfuge until the buildings were erected and the school was opened. A daughter of a banking empire, Katherine was steely, pragmatic, and determined.

She persisted, until her 77th year, when she suffered a stroke that would end her career. Mother Katherine retired to her sanctuary and spent the next twenty years in peace and intense prayer.

She died at the age of 97 on March 3, 1955. By the end of her life, Katherine Drexel had spent an estimated twenty-million dollars of her inheritance. She has been attributed to performing two miracles through prayer, one during her life, and another after death. She was beatified by Pope John Paul II in 1998, and canonized in 2000, becoming only the second U.S. citizen ever raised to sainthood.

Whether or not Katherine ever visited St. Joseph's Industrial School is unsure, although she was known for visiting her special projects. If she ever made the journey, or just provided the money, her contribution to the school has not been forgotten. The dormitories had originally been named St. Anthony and St. Dominic but were later renamed to honor the generous heiresses who had made the school a reality. The main school building is named for her, Drexel Hall. Another of the buildings is named Morrell for Louise Drexel Morrell, who also contributed a sizable portion of the donation.

Arch of St. Josephs with Chapel and Bell Tower behind

And the historic, now derelict, Chapel is St. Katherine's Chapel, built in 1896, a year after DeRuyter purchased the property.

Like Katherine Drexel, the Josephites believed that education was the cornerstone that must be laid in order to lift youth out of poverty. The mission of St. Joseph's Industrial School was to not only educate young African American boys, filling in the gaps of their nominal educational institutions, but also to teach them a vocation, such as carpentry, printing, or farming. The marriage of the Josephite Order with Katherine Drexel's vision was a marriage well made.

Essentially what DeRuyter created was a boarding school for middle school aged youth. The boys slept in the dormitories, ate their meals in the dining hall, took their classes in the same building where they slept, and played in the fields next to the school. They took Mass at the Chapel daily, though conversion to Catholicism was not a requirement. Aside from students of African American backgrounds, the school sometimes admitted a Latino student, and from one account of a former student, at least one white student attended.

The children were required to remain at St. Joseph's a minimum of three years, but not more than five years. While they could have visitors at the school, they were not allowed to return home except for holidays and the end of the school year. The family would sign a youngster or two up for the school, often brothers or cousins. Then the boys would be transported to Clayton, Delaware, where they would live until the end of the school year, when they were transported back to their homes. Early on it was a stipulation that the parents or guardians arranged the transportation. Later, the school would take the boys home by bus. Having good financial support, the tuition for the school was nominal. Parents were required to pay five dollars a month to repair clothing, shoes, school books, athletic equipment, and musical instruments. The young men were required to bring with them a supply of underwear and dress clothes for Mass. Work clothes and shoes were provided by the school.

Directly after the Civil War and at the turn of the 20th Century, the vast majority of African-Americans lived in rural areas. Thus, farming must have seemed a natural enterprise to teach the youth. However, from 1916 to 1970 the Great Migration was underway, a period when some six million African Americans immigrated away from the South and its poor economic climate and stifling Jim Crow laws, to urban areas in search of jobs and affordable housing (Great Migration).

With the advent of the two World Wars, industries, especially defense industries, had massive labor shortages. Thus, In the later decades of St. Josephs' Industrial School, the majority of the students hailed from mainly urban regions. The boys came from the inner cities of Philadelphia, Washington D.C, Baltimore, and New York City predominantly, although one lad lived as far away as Texas, and several boys hailed from the Carolinas.

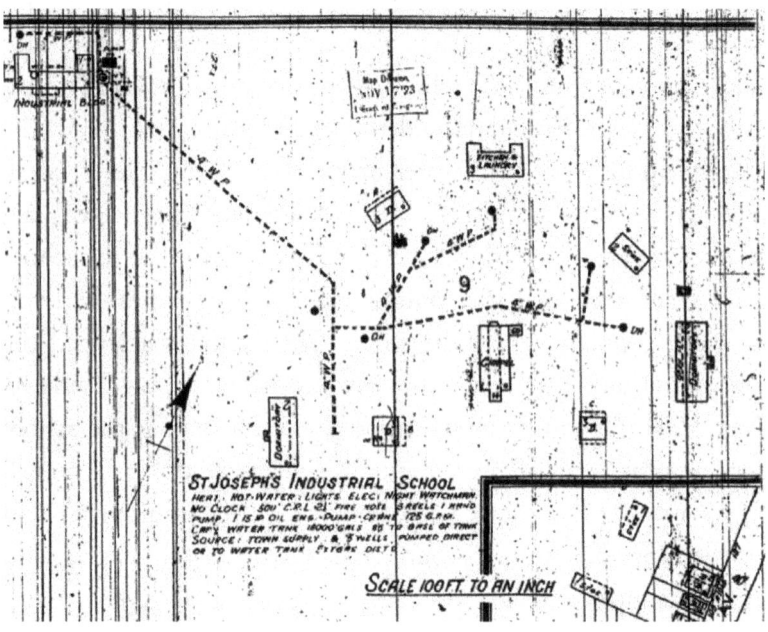

Platt Map of St. Josephs Industrial School

Arriving on a 400-acre farm in rural Delaware from the inner city, separated for the first time in their lives from family and friends, many of the boys had a steep and troubled adjustment period. Runaways were not uncommon, but most were caught and returned to the school where the brothers would kindly try to cajole them to stay. Apparently, a few of the more determined boys actually made it home.

Former St. Joseph's student, William Horton, said they teased each other about what clothes they wore. He laughingly said that you could tell where a boy was from by his fighting style. Apparently, the Philadelphians were known for nasty tussles and unscrupulous fighting techniques, and thus were taunted with refrains such as, "you want a fair one? you want a fair one?" (Horton)

For those that succeeded through the adjustment period, the boarding school started to represent a quintessential period in their lives. The gentlemen that I spoke with could recite the names of all the brothers by whom they had been taught and mentored. Many had made pilgrimages back to the school at one time or another to check up on the property and reminisce. To make a journey to Clayton, Delaware takes determination, as one doesn't just pass by Clayton on the road to anywhere else. For most, it appeared to be a significant turning point in their lives.

BARN AND PART OF HERD

The farm was fully functioning, raising crops. Corn, wheat, oats, soybeans, timothy grass and clover alfalfa, Sudan grass, white potatoes, sweet potatoes, cucumbers, and lettuce were all grown on the sprawling 400 acres. Hogs, 50 milk cows and numerous chickens provided food and eggs.

The farm not only provided food for the school, but the excess was sold to keep the institution solvent. The morning milk was sold for profit, the evening milk was used for drinking and to make butter. Fruits and vegetables were grown and preserved for year-round consumption.

Farm hands performed most of the heavy work, sowing the fields, and feeding the livestock. Boys that wanted to work with the animals were given that opportunity. Helping work the farm was considered more of a privilege than a right. Bringing in the hay was a communal event, culminating in a hay ride back to the school that the boys looked forward to yearly. At one time, the school even acquired two retired New York City police horses. These immense, but docile, creatures were the favorite beasts of not only the residents of the school, but also neighborhood children who were sometimes given the opportunity to take a lumbering ride around the paddock.

For years the school also printed a monthly newsletter. Subscriptions were sold for fifty-cents a year. The money was used to fund the school and generate further donations. The print shop became a major source of revenue up until the 1960's. A linotype machine was used for the printing, and an addressograph machine printed off the addresses for the thousands of people on the mailing list. The newsletter featured stories about the priests and brothers, their promotions, and movements. It also ran features on student life, the reading programs, the kids in the band, the baseball team, and the year the school took first place in state for basketball. The booklets still in existence offer a rare glimpse into the school and its functioning.

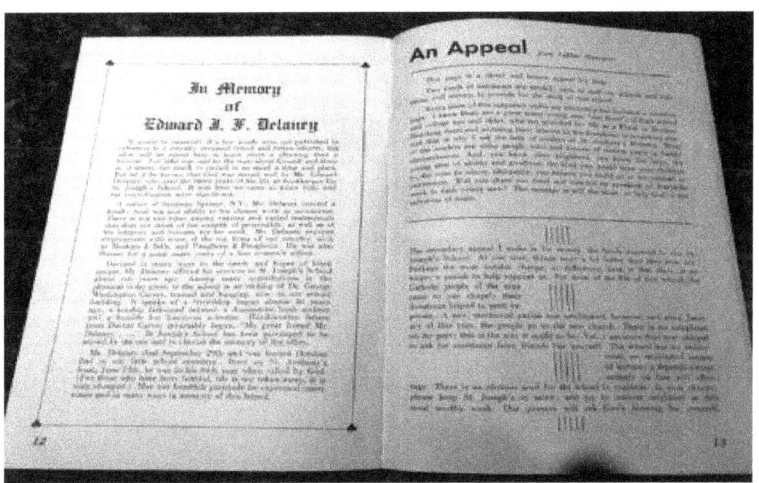

St. Joseph's publication An Appeal for funds

The Chapel functioned not only as a building for the school to use for morning Mass, but was also used by the St. Polycarp's Catholic congregation of Clayton and nearby Smyrna residents. St. Polycarp's held Mass on Sundays in the Chapel, but also hosted weddings and presumably funerals in the beautiful Italianate structure with its some 50 stained glass windows. In 1968 the St. Polycarp congregation moved to a newly built church in Smyrna, Delaware, presumably a structure with modern plumbing and better heating. When St. Polycarp decamped, they took their donation baskets with them. The St. Polycarp website offered an excellent overview of the arrangement between St. Joseph's Industrial school and the St. Polycarp Catholic Parish.

> Early in 1918, Bishop Monaghan decided to sell St. Polycarp's to the Centennial Methodist Episcopal Church and build a new church in Clayton. The Diocese purchased land on West Street, adjacent to the present-day Ewell's—St. Paul Methodist Church. However, due to the outbreak of World War I, the building plans were postponed and the Chapel at St. Joseph's Industrial School, in Clayton, which was established in 1895 by Reverend John A. DeRuyter, S.S.J. became the parish church. Meanwhile, the land that the diocese bought in Clayton was sold to the Methodist Church there.
>
> For the next fifty years this Josephite Missionary Society served the needs of the church and under their care great strides were made in solidifying Catholicism in upper Kent and lower New Castle Counties. Bishop Fitzmaurice was anxious to revive the Smyrna Parish of St. Polycarp's with a diocesan priest as pastor, but was prevented from doing so by World War II and the shortage of priests.

In 1963 Father Francis J. Tierney was appointed the first diocesan pastor. He continues to build community among Catholics of the area, using the facilities at St. Joseph's School in Clayton. Finally, on May 26, 1964, Bishop Hyles announced plans to build a new St. Polycarp's Church on South Street and Ransom Lane in Smyrna. The new parish opened its doors for services for the first time on January 20, 1968 and was solemnly dedicated by Bishop Mardaga on May 26, 1968 (St. Polycarp).

Not long after the St. Polycarp's Congregation decamped for modern plumbing, this edition of St. Anthony's Monthly indicated that St. Joseph's was under some severe financial stress, both from a lack of staffing, but also from a reliable funding source.
As the first point of Father Newsom's appeal, he asks specifically for such volunteers.
This page is a direct and honest appeal for help.
Two kinds of assistance are needed: men to staff our schools and missions, and money to provide for the work of this school.
Every issue of this magazine under my editorship has included a vocation page. I know there are a great many young men "out there," of high school and college age and older, who are qualified for life as a Priest or Brother, and that is why I ask the help of readers of St. Anthony's Monthly. Most of the readers are older people, men, and women of mature years in family circumstances. And, you know your neighbors, you know the boys, the young men of ability and goodness, the kind you would trust your children to, the ones to whom, ultimately, you believe you could go to for counsel or confession. Will you share our need and concern by speaking of Josephite work to such

young men? The message is still the same: to help God in the salvation of souls.

The secondary appeal I make is for money, the funds required to run St. Joseph's School. At one time, things were a lot better than they now are. Perhaps the most notable change, or difference here is that there is no longer a parish to help support us. For most of the life of this school the Catholic people of the area came to our Chapel; their donations helped to meet expenses. A new, territorial parish was established, however, and since January of this year, the people go to the new church. There is no complaining on my part; this is the way it ought to be. Yet, I am more than ever obliged to ask for assistance from friends like yourself. The school has no endowment, no established means of income, it depends almost entirely on free will offerings. There is an obvious need for the school to continue. In your charity keep St. Joseph's in mind' and try to interest neighbors in this most worthy work. Our prayers will ask God's blessing for yourself.

The St. Polycarp congregation moved locations in 1968, St. Joseph's officially closed their doors in 1972, only 5 years later.

The actual teaching and vocational training were done by the brothers, a rare and dedicated group of young men that would give up their lives in dedication to the church and the church's mission. They were considered a caste underneath the priesthood. Yet, these were the young men who taught the young boys their lessons, provided extra-curricular activities in the afternoons and slept with the youngsters in the evenings to make sure no chicanery was unfolding.

The boarding school and the town were quite insulated from one another. Clayton as a whole is predominantly Caucasian while the boarding school youth were almost completely comprised of African American youth. Also, the grounds were 400 acres large, offered a fully functioning farm, grounds for sports and play and even a pond in back for swimming and ice skating. The boys rarely left the school grounds, and when they did, it was to take short forays into Clayton or nearby Dover for special events. There was one article in the *St. Anthony's Monthly* indicating that the boys participated in a Clayton 4th of July parade one year. Such twining of the school with the neighboring town, however, appears to have been rather rare.

The school and Clayton residents co-existed for 82 years in mostly harmonious conditions, and the school educated upwards of 7,000 boys. Still, what went on at the school was a complete mystery to everyone except for those who attended. An internet search brought me to a blog post by a woman who lived in Clayton most of her life. On the blog I found the names and email addresses of three gentlemen that had attended St. Joseph's and could provide me with the missing information.

One of the first things I wanted to do when writing this book was get into the history of St. Joseph's. Not the bare history, which amounts to a lot of facts and figures. A certain number of boys attended in a certain year under the tutelage of Father John…or Ralph…or Charles. What I really wanted to know was what was it *like* to attend St. Joseph's Industrial School as a boy, as an African-American boy, at a time when the two races were mostly segregated? I wanted to see into that time capsule and find out what it meant to St. Joseph's Industrial School. Could I find someone who would actually talk to me? I was nervous when I made the calls, I won't lie. But the three gentlemen I interviewed were marvelous. They made the boarding school come to life. The brothers who mostly ran the schools oversaw their charges 24 -hours a day with dignity and kindness. They taught the boys, fed the boys, kept the boys occupied, entertained the boys, and finally gave the boys long-lasting values that resonated throughout the years of their lives.

Thom Akens,
Former student of St. Joseph's Industrial School
(Attended 1955-1958)

Thom Aikens with classmates at a St. Joseph Industrial School reunion. Photo provided by Thom Aikens

Thom recounts being sent to St. Joseph's. "At the beginning it was sad, because I wasn't from Delaware, I was from Washington DC. I was sent to St. Joseph's not as a punishment, but as a way to keep me out of trouble. I was from southwest Washington. There were about five or six kids in the neighborhood. We ran around together, played games together (Aikins)." One of their games was to shoot ball bearings with home-made slingshots, a game that would eventually land the boys in some trouble.

Obviously, a ball bearing shot from a slingshot with force might seriously hurt someone. Apparently, the police thought so as well. One day when he was folding newspapers for his friend who had a paper route, two police officers approached Thom and asked him if he had a slingshot. Thom replied affirmatively and showed the officers his toy. They then took possession of the slingshot and gave Thom a ride down to the police station where they called his mother to pick him up.

Thom's mother, probably fearing that her son was growing up in a rough neighborhood, told him quite pointedly, not long after the incident, that he was being sent away to a boarding school, the same one the boy down the street had been sent a year before. His mother told Thom that she wouldn't let him get, "Mixed up with a bunch of hooligans." Thom was St. Joseph's bound.

"In September of 1955 I went to St. Joseph's Boarding School. There were about 60 boys in the school." While St. Joseph's was a Catholic run school, at this time the school was being run by lay people. A Mr. Govier (pronounced Go Fair) was the principal at the time. While there were Priests, Brothers and nuns on the property, Mr. Govier had the daily job of actually running the school.

Unfortunately, Mr. Govier had sticky fingers and was caught with money that was left by the parents for their children to buy snacks and other items. Mr. Govier and his sticky fingers were given the boot not too long after Thom arrived.

The running of the school was then transferred back to the Priests and Brothers. Father Patrick took over the operations of the school. Teaching and supervision of the boys usually fell to the brothers. "There was a Brother James, a Brother

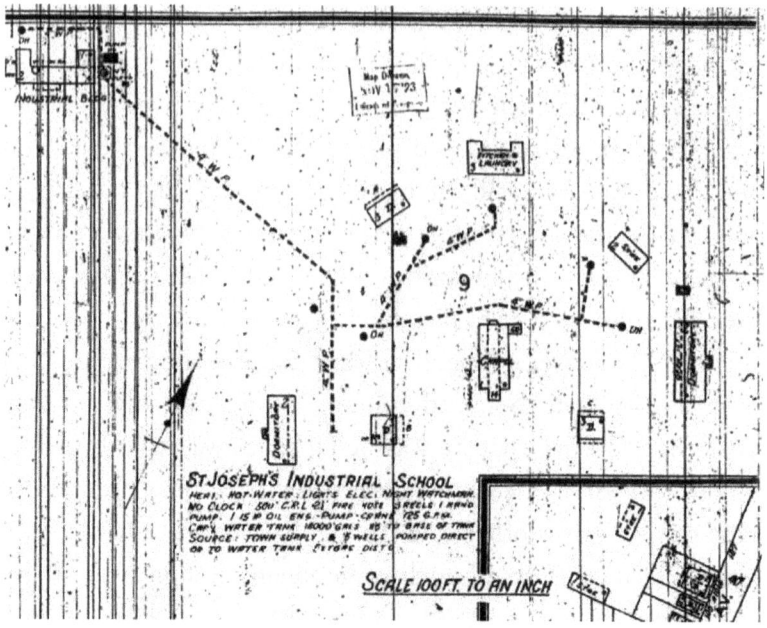

Old Plat Map of the School Grounds. Many of the building listed on the Plat no longer stand, while new buildings have taken their place.

Earl, a Brother Charles, a Brother Lawrence and a Brother Kent." What struck me about Thom's account was the fact that, all these long years later, he could still list the names of the brothers as if he'd only been there last week. It attests to the fact that these men really impacted a young man far from home.

The priests and nuns lived in a house by themselves and actually had very little interaction with the students. When Thom arrived, there were five or six nuns living on the property, but they moved away not long after. I've not been able to ascertain what the actual functioning of the nuns on the property was, as they appeared to have little to no interaction with the boys at the school. Again, the daunting task of watching over every aspect of the students' lives fell to the brothers.

Thom recalls that the class size for any one grade was around 20 students, and the entire student body numbered only around 80.

"There were boys in the school that were bullies. That's to be expected. My mother sent me a care package, and I made the mistake of opening it in the dormitory, and everyone saw what was in it. So, I put it in my locker and went to bed. The next morning, I got up and went to my locker. The lock was gone, and needless to say, the care package was gone also."

Despite that, there were very few fights among the boys, Thom recalls. There were two dorms on the property. As one came into the main gate there was a dorm to the left and a dorm to the right named St. Anthony's and St. Dominic's. These wooden structures no longer exist, having been replaced in 1959 by a brick building which housed everything, now named Drexel Hall. The older boys lived in the dorm on the right, the younger boys the dorm on the left. The kitchen was located to the back of the Church in a separate wooden structure, which has also disappeared in time, but can be seen on the 1923 Platt Map. The kitchen and laundry building appear to be located where Drexel is located today.

Thom admitted that occasionally boys, homesick for their families and friends, attempted to run away from the school. Clayton, Delaware is a relatively small community. For boys familiar with the teeming activity of a large city, it must have felt like being dropped off in the middle of nowhere. "Just a little way away from the school was a railroad track. Boys would sometimes run over to the railroad track and try to get away. A few hours later the [Brothers] would bring them back. The [boys] didn't know where they were and they would just get lost."

The farmhands and the custodian lived in an old wooden building that had once been a dormitory. The building was the only remaining wooden structure left from when the school had first opened in 1896. Two months before Thom left, the old dormitory structure burned down in a blaze that could be seen five miles away. One of the farmhands had been smoking in bed and started the fire. He died in the blaze, though everyone else managed to get out. The fire was detected at around 1:00 a.m., and the Brothers woke the boys and took them outside and had them stand in a group safely away from the flames, where they watched the building succumb to the inevitable.

Thom recalled the beginning of rock and roll in 1956. The boys would sneak to the kitchen door to listen to the music. "There were certain songs on the Hit Parade that we were not allowed to listen to, because they were considered dirty." When the Brothers caught the boys listening at the door, they would shoo them away.

To the left of the church there stood a small house that was converted into a library. There weren't a lot of books, but they had a record player. The boys would go there to listen to music.

Thom recalled a festive event in the gymnasium when he got his first taste of something completely new. Brother Charles, who was of Italian descent and hailed from New Jersey, made pizzas for the boys. Thom had never seen a pizza, and he mistook his slice for cake. Biting into it, he found out differently. He approached Brother Charles and asked, "What is this? It isn't cake, but it's good. Brother Charles said, 'It's pizza.'" Thom liked the new concoction.

The Brothers not only taught classes and planned activities. They also watched over the dormitories at night. To the rear of the dormitory was a room for the Brothers. When Brother Kent moved into the dormitory, he had a hole cut in the wall between his room and the dorm room. He put a window in, and hung a curtain. In that way he could catch boys trying to sneak out of bed at night. "Then he'd come out and take care of you."

"He'd say, 'What you doing getting out of bed?'"

"Brother Kent, I'm just going to the bathroom."

"All right, you go to the bathroom, and then you get back in that bed. I don't want to see you until tomorrow morning. "

The boys were assigned certain chores. One week they might be assigned to wash dishes. Another week they might help with the cooking in the kitchen or cleaning of the dorms. Thom recalled an incident, that may have been racially charged, by one of the residents in the nearby community. This particular week Thom was working in the kitchen with another boy from Long Island. The Brother instructed the boy to take the trash outdoors to the trash bin. It was around six or seven o'clock in the evening.

"He went out the door, and the next thing I know he ran back into the kitchen hollering and screaming." Someone had come around the back of the building and attacked the boy from behind. He never got a chance to see who had attacked him.

Not knowing who the assailant might be, the Brothers put all the students on lockdown in the classrooms on the first floor of the dormitory. The boys were looking out the window when the night watchman came by and entered the kitchen. The boys mistook the night watchman for the assailant, and panic ensued before the night watchman identified himself. The Brothers came in and told the boys to calm down. It was a tense situation for several days, but no other attacks were made. The assailant was never discovered.

Thom recalls that punishments for misbehavior were not severe. Often it was just an injunction of, "no dessert for you tonight."

"The Brothers weren't hard on us, but they kept us in line."

According to Thom, it was the bullies and thieves among them that had to be watched and punished. Aside from the hoodlums, most co-existed peacefully.

There was one incident of a very serious nature that affected the entire school. It was reported that a few of the older boys were molesting the younger students. Brother James, an authoritarian, according to Thom, locked all the boys down in the dormitories and didn't allow them to go out.

"We got up and put our clothes on, but we had to stay by our beds. We couldn't talk to anybody."

The lockdown began at 8:00 in the morning. By 9:00 a.m. the boys were getting restless, not understanding what was going on. They were finally released at 10, when they were told to assemble on the playing field.

Brother James told the boys about the abuse, and told them all that such behaviors would not be tolerated. The boys responsible for the molestations were then pointed out. Using fists, the Brothers then beat the boys in front of the entire assembly. Such a public spectacle made an impression on young Thom. However, Thom felt the public beatings were deserved, and no further incidents occurred after that.

Their day began at 8:00 a.m. The first hour of the day was spent in Chapel, followed by breakfast. They then spent the rest of the day in class. At 3:00 p.m., they were released to play outside. Dinner was at five.

Down a gravel road toward the back of the school grounds was a spring fed pond. Every spring the pond was dammed and would fill up with water, and it would become the boys' favorite swimming hole. They shared the swimming hole with workers from the canning factory, who would use the pond for swimming when the boys weren't there, and the boys used the hole when the canning factory employees weren't around. Sometimes local kids would use the pond for liaisons, and the boys sometimes interrupted such trysts accidentally.

The Brothers also organized sporting events. Brother Earl assembled a basketball team of which Thom was a member. There was only one problem, Thom had no idea how to play basketball.

"I had never played basketball before in my life, but I joined the team." Brother Earl arranged for the basketball game in Dover. "So, we got on the bus Saturday morning to go to play. So, the game begins, and Brother Earl calls me out to go on the court. So, I stepped out on the court, and someone threw me a basketball. The whistle blows and we're starting to play." Not having any idea how the game was played, Thom stood there with the basketball in his hands stunned. "I'm standing there holding the ball. I didn't dribble the ball; I didn't run with the ball. I just stood there. I saw the other boys running down the court, but I didn't know what they were running for. Finally, Brother Earl called me out and told me to sit down. 'Sit down, sit down,'" he said in disgust. I've never played basketball since." It was the beginning and end of Thom's basketball career.

During Thom's final year at the school, the Brothers decided to try something different, probably thinking they'd install some discipline of a more martial nature. They tried to transition into a military school. All the boys were put in khaki uniforms and were made to march in formation to class functions. Ranks were assigned by age, with the older boys having the higher ranks. The older boys were essentially in charge of the younger boys. "They would march us from the dining hall to the school and back again." This only lasted a single year, before it was given up.

Obviously, the boys attended services daily; however, most were not Catholic and didn't know the strictures of the faith.

The second year Thom was at school, his younger cousin Marshall was brought up to attend as well. "When it came time for communion, the Priest started passing out communion." Thom's cousin went up, kneeled down and received the sacrament. "I said, Marshall, you're not supposed to be up there. He said, 'well, they were passing out food, and I thought I'd get some.'" Thom eventually was baptized in the Chapel. The Priests didn't press their religion on the boys; it was left to the boys to make their own decision.

Homesick during his first year of school, Thom hatched a plan. At Christmas break he loaded all of his possessions into a foot locker and took it all home. He was hoping that his mother would allow him to stay. They brought all the boys home on a bus to Union Station, where they met their parents. "I dragged the foot locker off the bus, and my mother showed up." She welcomed her son with hugs and kisses. But when Thom went to drag the foot locker to the car she was surprised. "Well, you toted that thing home, you're going to tote it back to school at the end of the two weeks." At the end of the two weeks Thom hauled said foot locker back to school. Having learned his lesson the hard way, when he returned home for summer break, he traveled much more lightly.

Thom concurred that the students were kept fairly insulated from the residents of Clayton and nearby Dover. They only rarely left the school grounds. In fact, the basketball game in Dover is the only trip off the school grounds that Thom remembers. This parallels other accounts of residents and former students. The boys attended Chapel services, but only when the residents weren't using the building.

The school also hosted a summer camp. The boys that remained for summer camp all moved into one dormitory. They didn't have classes during the summer, but the camp provided activities. The boys swam at their favorite swimming hole, played games, had campfires, and enjoyed themselves immensely. Brother Earl was an avid photographer, and taught the boys the skill.

St. Joseph's was only for grades five through eight. When his time at St. Joseph's ended, Thom returned to Washington D.C. He attended his local high school for one year and then enlisted in the Air Force. After a career in the Air Force which included a tour of Vietnam and a position at the Pentagon he retired. He has fond memories of St. Joseph's, so fond that he returned to the property for a visit with his wife. The dormitory on the left that housed the older boys was gone, as was their dining hall and library. He was amazed at the renovations that have transformed his once boyhood home.

William Horton,

Former student of St. Joseph's Industrial School (Attended 1959-1964)

William started at St. Joseph's in 1959 after growing up in Washington D.C. When he started at St. Joseph's, he was already two years behind, but he already knew much of the curriculum. "It was the best thing to ever happen to me. I learned discipline there. The school was really good for a lot of us. For me especially, it removed me from the environment I was growing up in. I wasn't doing well in school. My mind was not into school. I would go to school and sit there and watch the clock waiting for the time I could get out of there. And then I was kind of mischievous. But St. Joseph's changed a lot of us. It gave us something to do. And we had a lot of [extra-curricular] activities. There was basketball, baseball, football, and the Catholic School organization." William's older brother was a two-time marble champion in the state of Delaware.

Undoubtedly, the hardest part of boarding school life was being absent from family back home. William recalled the end of his first year when the bus dropped him off in D.C. He ran home, came in the back door, and ran upstairs to see his grandmother. Grandma had been raising the boy from the age of three, and they were close. After his second year at school the homecomings weren't as joyous for William. The same year as the Kennedy assassination, Grandma passed away. William was 13. "Going home that time was a little bit different. Grandma wasn't there...."

Homesickness affected many of the boys. William remembered when six of the students decided they were going to run away. They apparently were planning it, because the news spread among the other children, but not the Brothers. The six actually made their escape, making the journey back home to Baltimore and Washington D.C. William didn't know whether they followed the train tracks that ran next to the school property, or whether they hitch hiked, probably the latter was the more likely route.

He, like Thom, denied that the Brothers were unusually harsh in their discipline. He recalled only one instance that happened before he arrived when a Brother made an advance on one of the boys. Apparently, he was dealt with, as William heard of no other illicit behavior.

He remembered that everything that happened spread quickly through the gossip network. William did recall a situation that involved his older brother, who also attended the school. The Brothers roughed his brother up, but William recounted unequivocally that the boy deserved every bit of the beating.

"If you got wrong, they straightened you out. It was an old Catholic school, they were old-fashioned. I guess some of them were war vets. I guess they ended up there because of what they'd seen [during their service]. But they were really cool." William had his favorites, Brother Thomas, and Brother Eugene who he said were extremely comical.

They did have a holly stick (and here in his story William laughed) with which they whacked the boys' behinds occasionally. Apparently, the implement wasn't much of a disciplinary horror. "They would bring out the holly stick, which was just a short stick, and whack us three or four times on the butt. It was nothing serious. One time they whupped the whole school." One of the boys got spray paint on the stage curtains, and the culprit didn't come forward to confess.

Because they couldn't ascertain the name of the painter, they decided instead on group punishment. "They took all four classrooms and just lined us up in the hallway." The Brothers lined up all the boys in the hallway and switched them all. They boys thought it was hilarious. "We were laughing even though it stung a little bit when they hit us with the stick. But they were very good people."

William also remembered the attempt at transforming into a military school. They made his parents buy him khaki pants and shirts. "Where my parents got the spats for over the shoes, I have no idea." The school even had an Air Force service member come in from the Dover Base to teach the boys how to drill. It lasted only his first year, and then they eliminated it.

He recalled much the same schedule of Chapel in the mornings followed by school with a two-hour play period either outside on the field or in the gymnasium. After play, the boys were taken back to the classroom for a study hall period and then back to the dormitories to play games or watch T.V. until bedtime.

William's days were also taken up with farming chores. He volunteered for farm work, positions that the boys would kill for, according to him. He said he was fortunate enough to be one of the few students to actually work the farm. He worked mucking stalls and playing with the cats. His particular job was working with the newborn Holstein calves. He usually worked after school and on the weekends around the barns. In a competition with a local 4-H club, he was given 50 small chickens to raise. He lost two of his chicks and the rest didn't weigh very much, so he didn't rise to Chicken Champion, but he enjoyed the experience.

One of the Brothers that worked the farm got sick and was out for a couple of weeks convalescing. It became William's job to do the early morning milking. He slept in the infirmary during this time, presumably so he wouldn't wake the other boys on his early morning forays. For two weeks he got up with the sun at 5:00 AM and milked the cows. He got kicked hard in the chest once by a cow he'd come to milk. But he learned his way around farm animals, how to tap them and speak gently to them so they didn't spook. The farm had a working collie that herded- independently - the cows in from the pasture every morning. The dog was an incredible herder, according to William, a one-dog, cow herding machine.

The farm hands planted yearly crops of hay, barley, corn, and alfalfa. When it was haying time, he said, the entire school got involved loading and unloading the hay bales. It was a lark for the boys that didn't work the farm. They thought of it as a hay ride, riding the bales back in from the fields.

William recalled community involvement with the town of Clayton included competitions and marching in the town's parade. The band played the school's song, and the boys marched and sang. "St. Joseph's is our school.... The sons are we. We are true to the golden rule of faith, hope and charity...." They even won the award one year. Father Caludet tried to interest the boys in singing in a choir, but the attempt failed. Middle school aged boys didn't have much interest in choir singing, apparently.

Their interests ran more toward sports. Aside from football, basketball, and baseball, the school also competed in track. They would attend field meets in Wilmington, where William tried the long jump and running. But he wasn't destined to be a track star.

William remembered that during the Christmas season, the boys performed plays for the visiting Luciens. These Luciens would attend the performance, and they brought Christmas gifts for the boys. After the festivities everyone would celebrate with a feast. None of the boys knew what they were being given until they opened them, at which time they would barter with one another for a present they preferred. One year William remembers he received a shirt and tie. But what he really wanted was a small race car that another boy had received. They were able to make an amicable swap, and William got his race car.

Every Friday of the Easter season the boys performed the stations of the cross. Throughout the rest of the year, they often performed novenas where the boys were marched from one area to another on the campus where the priests would say prayers.

William's aunt had something to do with the faculty, although he couldn't recall exactly what the position was. When they built the new dormitories, his aunt was there with a shovel for the initial groundbreaking. He saw it on a video years after, and identified his aunt as the one who turned the shovel.

William and his brother actually lived in the new dormitories of Drexel Hall, as the older dormitories had been abandoned. Drexel, as it's named today, was built to be an all-purpose building with classrooms on one side of the building, a large central gymnasium and stage area in the center, and dormitories on the other side of the building. All were accessible by a long central hallway which ran the entire length of the building.

"I was in the new dormitory one day looking out the back window." The view out of the window brought the song "America the Beautiful" to his mind. "Because what I saw, when the wind was blowing and that barley was waving… it was amber. Amber waves of grain, just like in that song. Whenever I hear that song, that's what I see in my mind. It was beautiful."

He also had fond memories of the swimming pond, although he said he almost drowned there once. Every so often a water moccasin might swim past, which gave the boys a scare. Apparently, the pond was quite deep when full. William estimated that it might have been 10 feet at its deepest point. It was also cold all year round, suggesting that the pond was actually spring fed. On his visit back to the school a couple of years ago, he noted that he visited the old pond, and was disheartened by what he saw. The pond has been sorely neglected. There's now a tree growing up in the middle of it, and shrubs and weeds have overtaken the edges. No one swims there anymore.

The swimming hole as it looks today overgrown and disused

During summer camp, he recalled that the school provided two rafts which the boys used to traverse the waterways. "Summer camp was fun." He recalled a time for games and swimming and no stuffy classrooms. The school had apparently built four small cabins at the pond, and the boys camped out in the cabins often during their summer breaks. Camp fires and storytelling abounded.

He recalled a summer when one of the boys decided it would be good sport to throw a hatchet at the trees. To discipline the boy, one of the brothers took him into the school's cemetery and tied the boy to the cross in the center of the cemetery. Luckily the lad wasn't frightened, and everyone had a good laugh over the punishment.

William returned to the school a few years ago, while the school was on break. In 1995, his oldest daughter was graduating from high school in Washington D.C. William drove from California to Washington D.C. for the graduation. While in the area he drove up to Delaware to visit his old haunt, bringing his wife along for the ride. He stopped at the building, which had been the habitat of the Priests and Brothers. He knocked, not knowing who might still be in residence, if anyone. A man opened the door. The two stood looking at each other in amazement.

"It was Brother Charles," who had run the laundry for the school. Charles informed William that the Catholic ministry was selling the property, which had officially closed in 1972. "I just felt so bad when I heard that." Apparently, Charles and a couple of the other Brothers were there to see to the official closing and turning of the school over to the new owners, Providence Creek Academy.

After his visit, William told his brother about the Chapel being abandoned, but that the Chapel was still looking relatively intact. He said his brother, who also attended St. Joseph's, started to cry. William was perplexed and asked why his brother was so moved. "He said, 'I was baptized in that church.'" And so, the indelible memories that still move grown men to tears.

Now retired, William spent a career in the Marine Corps and then became a Merchant Marine. "When at times we were out to sea, and I had a lot of time to think, I would often remember St. Joseph's and how much fun we had. It's so beautiful at night on the water, watching the phosphoric trail of the dolphins that followed the ship and tracing the paths of the comets." This is the time he reminisced about his boyhood and his fondest memories, many of which included St. Joseph's, its brotherhood, its peace, and its amber waves of grain.

Row one: Oscar Little, Rudolph Bradshaw, Father Charles Brown, Jerome Barber, Larry Covington (became a sportscaster in DC), Father Veale.
Row two: Larry Underwood, Leon Hatton, William Holley, Kincaid.
Row three: Gibbs, unknown, Dunnington, unknown.
Row four: Anderson, Anthony Towe, Albert Jackson.
Row five: John Kennedy, Harvey Martin, Rodney Harrison.
Row six: George Kirby.

Leon Hatton,

Former student of St. Joseph's Industrial School
(Attended 1959-1961)

I didn't find Leon, he found me, or rather answered a request I had left on a blog by a local author. Such is the power of the community of St. Joseph's Industrial School.

Leon was growing up in Washington D.C. with his mother and his grandmother. His father was absent, and Leon was growing up without much discipline and no male influences. He was living a rather wild existence according to his own accounts. He mentioned that he had already attempted to run away from home a couple times. His two sisters attended a Catholic Boarding School in Pennsylvania named Holy Providence which was an all-girls' school. When Leon's mother found out about St. Joseph's, she must have seen the school as the necessary answer to her son's intractable behavior. Leon was sent there the very next school year. He only attended the school for two years, seventh and eighth grades, but he said that those two years had a profound effect on the man that he would eventually become.

Leon arrived in the fall of 1959; he was 11. He admitted that he had never had a routine nor been expected to fulfill any responsibilities around the house. Thus, it took young Leon a few weeks to adjust to expectations from the Brothers that he would be responsible for at least some of the duties required for his own upkeep; schedules and duties were new to the young man.

Upon arrival, young Leon shirked his duties. He admitted that he acted out, getting into fisticuffs with several of the other boys. What more, he was winning those fights, which was earning him a reputation and a following amongst the younger boys, swelling the young man's head with thoughts of prowess.

As the earlier testimonials suggested, the boys were assigned chores such as washing dishes, washing and waxing floors, doing laundry; all the things necessary to keep the school clean and running. Young Leon decided that chores were beneath him. He would show up for his daily jobs but wouldn't participate.

This came to the attention of Brother Lawrence, the Dormitory Master of St. Anthony's. Lawrence was undoubtedly worried that their new student was turning into a trouble-making force, and decided an earnest, heart-to-heart discussion was needed.

"Brother Lawrence sat me down and talked to me. He didn't beat me or anything, he just talked to me. He just *talked* to me. He was very firm. It was the first form of discipline from a man I had ever received." Leon said the experience moved him to tears. "I was very fortunate at that point in my life to have a man, a male figure in my life, that was going to sit me down and talk to me. It came to me at just the right time [in my life]."

Leon said his days were full. The children were awakened early to wash up and dress. Then they would form a line and walk to Mass. Following Mass, the boys would stand outside the church for a flag raising ceremony, followed by breakfast and class. There was a play period in the afternoons followed by a study hall, which he utilized to keep his grades predominantly in the A's.

In class, Leon excelled. After early academic success whetted his interest, he was able to maintain an A average all the way through the rest of his time there, graduating second in his class. He was able to achieve success, and that gave him confidence in his abilities that he had previously lacked.

Leon was also able to get one of the vaunted farm worker positions. He was assigned to taking care of the chickens, feeding them daily and collecting eggs. Once a month they had to buy feed for the chickens, and Leon would ride along in the truck with Brother George who ran the farm, to purchase the chicken feed. Sometimes they would have to take a few pigs in the truck to the slaughter house. "It really was a working farm," Leon noted.

They had a lot of time to play. Marbles and handball were favorites. There were the sports teams, but Leon was small and wasn't really competitive. He became the score keeper for the basketball team. He also remembers swimming in the pond followed by meals of barbecued hotdogs, and hayrides in the fall.

A small group of boys took a class in electronics. The assignment was to build their own radios. The boys worked diligently at their radios, soldering and placing components. This was the era of the tube, and the boys had to learn circuitry. Leon eventually finished his radio. With a feeling of accomplishment, he plugged the radio in…and it blew up. Ironically, later he would go on to actually work in electronics, not letting that exploding radio cause him too much dismay. Such was the power of St. Joseph's that it taught a young man a skill that would eventually become a career, and the temerity to try again even after his first attempt ended explosively.

Father Charles Brown inspecting the eggs with an unknown farm worker and one of St. Joseph's young apprentices

Leon was at St. Joseph's when the boys moved from the frame wood buildings to the all-encompassing building now named Drexel, for the patroness that made the school possible. In the late 50's this building must have revolutionized the school. Whereas before a wood building housed the dining hall, another the library, two more the dormitories, and yet another for classrooms, this building held everything in one location. And it had the added bonus that it was far less likely to go down in a fiery conflagration, as so many of the other buildings had done in the past.

Sometimes life wasn't so idyllic. Leon remembered two of the farm workers – students – got into an argument that became a fist fight and then grew deadly. One of the boys grabbed a farm implement and hit the other boy on the head, badly injuring him. The injured boy went to the hospital, and his attacker was expelled.

When he graduated Leon took two awards, a Farm Achievement Medal and a St. Anthony Medal for the most promising student. Larry Covington, valedictorian, was the student with whom Leon competed for grades. Larry went on to become a sportscaster on a Washington D.C. station in the 80's. Seeing his old school chum giving the nightly sports updates must have been a gratifying experience.

Leon knew Father Charles Brown, who was featured in the picture with the farm hand examining the eggs, and the group shot with the boys on the steps. Both photos were found in the now abandoned Chapel and later scanned by Janet. Father Brown officiated at Mass and Leon would see him there. He said Brown was kind, as everyone was, but beyond that he really didn't know him well. Father Brown is one of the priests that has been witnessed walking the halls of St. Joseph's, now First State Military Academy, long after he departed the school.

I asked Leon what made the school such a powerful force in his life, and he unequivocally said discipline. Not the discipline of a belt on a back side, but the discipline of a routine, and being held accountable for one's actions. These were the experiences that formed the then boy into a young man.

"I think it was the discipline. I didn't have any type of formal routine at home. The Brothers gave me that. It wasn't ideal, no one is perfect, and we were just boys. It also helped us learn how to get along with other people. It was a small microcosm of the world." A small microcosm of the world that was safe and supportive and enjoyable, where a boy could be a boy, discover his strengths, form friendships, run, play, swim, ride a horse, take a hayride, roast hotdogs. And watch the amber waves of grain outside their classroom. All the sons of loving Brothers who would never themselves have sons.

None of this, however, answers the question as to why St. Joseph's Industrial School, A.K.A. Providence Creek Academy, A.K.A. First State Military Academy, has earned such a reputation for being haunted. We're taught to think of a haunted location as being a location that has a long reputation of death and adversity. Certainly, the property has seen its share of tragedy over the years. From the untimely death of Father De Ruyter, to the deaths of several Priests and Brothers over time, the property has seen its share of death.

Fire engulfs one of the wooden structures on the property. Eventually the school would suffer 6 fires and would rebuild all the structures using brick.

Adding into the equation of several tragedies, six of the original wooden buildings burned down. Wood buildings, heated with wood stoves, tended to go up in flames. And so, they did. One farm hand died when the Farm Hands Dormitory burned down, the result of a fatal cigarette smoked in bed. One priest also perished in a fire when the former governor's mansion burned. Realizing, finally, that such fires were inevitable, the school eventually started rebuilding using brick instead. Hence the three remaining school buildings on the property all hail from the 1960's. The Chapel is the only original remaining St. Joseph's structure, and without needed maintenance, it's doubtful it will stand very much longer, despite its status on the National Record of Historic Properties.

A VIEW OF OUR SWIMMING POOL

The beloved swimming pond, now little more than a drainage hole.

The beloved swimming pond claimed the life of one child, a son of a school employee, who drowned. The pond, during the swimming season, was quite deep, and other near misses occurred as well.

To the rear of the property, nestled amongst a forest, is the small cemetery that became the final resting place of eight Priests and three Brothers along with several lay people from the surrounding community. The graves include a few children and two infants. Perhaps not all of the cemetery's inhabitants are resting as peacefully as intended.

INSIDE VIEW — ST. JOSEPH'S CHURCH

The Chapel at its finest. Now the building is mainly empty, the pews having been sold off, the statues stored in the basement.

The school shut its doors to students in 1972 amidst the cries for desegregation. I'm guessing, with the lack of funds plaguing the school and the political climate, the Catholic church felt that operating a school only for African-American, inner-city boys was considered at the time to be distasteful. So, such decisions are made during political unrest that seem in tune with the times, but really are deleterious in the end. No longer would inner-city boys get a chance to ride a horse, milk a cow, ride a hay wagon or see those amber waves shifting in the wind.

After 80 and some odd years of shaping the lives of young men, the Church closed the doors, turned the keys…and left. It became just another remarkable institution that didn't survive the wrecking ball of political correctness, a wrecking ball that eliminates all in its path without preamble or foresight.

The Chapel before the drop-ceiling was installed.

The property wasn't resold until 1999. Throughout those long 27 years, it sat mostly abandoned. Several congregations used the Chapel for a short duration.

Otherwise, the Chapel stood empty. The pews and the main altar were eventually sold off. The once grand structure is now mainly empty, adorned only by its walls of stained glass. A drop ceiling was installed at some point that covered the original wood beams, hiding the original architect's grand design.

The three brick buildings; Drexel Hall, Morrell Hall, and St. Michael's, were occasionally used for spiritual retreats and prayer centers. But mostly they were abandoned as well.

A caretaker took care of the grounds and kept the vandals out. The halls and dormitories, so often filled with the laughter and chatter of boys, were eerily silent, and the desks where boys took their studies lay in their neat rows unused. The beds in the dormitories remained unslept in, the lockers empty. The gymnasium creaked and cracked with the changing of the weather and the blowing of the wind. No boys now played basketball, or practiced plays on the stage. In the building where the priests lived, their belongings remained, although they had long since departed.

During the intermittent years of silence, apparently some of the former inhabitants decided to move back in. While no one I spoke with from the St. Joseph's Industrial School Days ever recalled any unsettling activity from when the school operated, the Providence Creek Academy Charter School certainly started to experience interlopers from the past almost immediately. Over the years of investigating the paranormal, I've noticed that abandoned buildings seem to attract paranormal hangers-on. Abandoned buildings with their silent, empty rooms offer a sort of peace and tranquility that appears to attract those that loved the buildings in the first place.

Within, they can dwell in anonymity, reliving their happier days in quiet repose. What is really unique about the St. Joseph's Industrial School closing is that when the Priests and Brothers closed the buildings, they left everything in place. As mentioned earlier, the desks remained, with the papers and pencils on them. The chalkboards had the last lesson still chalked in place. The priests not only left the beds made and dinnerware on the table, they also left many personal items behind.

It must have seemed that the next school day was about to begin, only it never did. While the possessions remained, the children were gone, and the long quiet years spanned out indefinitely…until they didn't. Suddenly the quietude was disturbed. There were children again, in the halls, in the rooms, playing basketball in the gymnasium, dancing in the Chapel. The past had come full circle, as it has a habit of doing, and St. Joseph's woke up and began to live again.

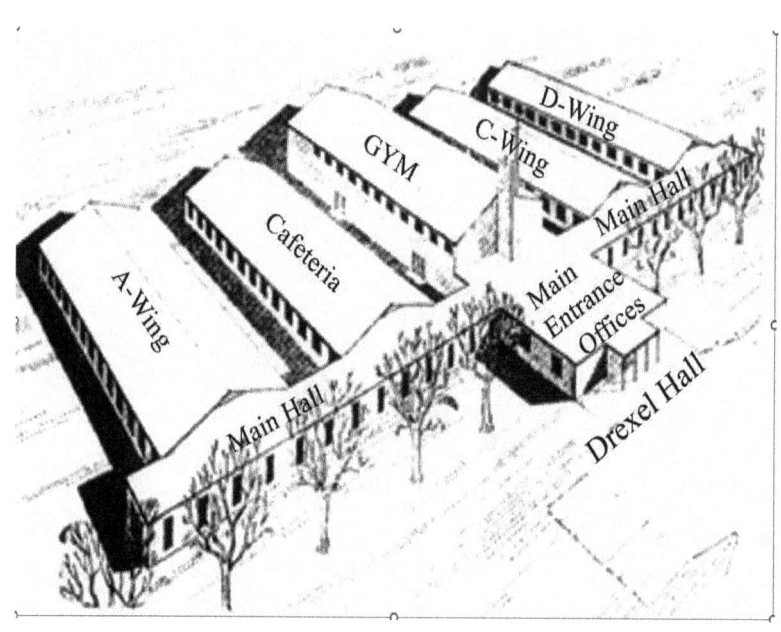

Drexel Hall: What had been dorm large dorm rooms in C and A-Wing were converted into classrooms. The original gym remains, built around by the wings of the school.

Chapter Two:
Providence Creek Academy

Chuck Taylor,
St. Joseph's Foundation Founding Board Member / Managing Director/ Head of School for Providence Creek Academy Charter School

In the writing of this book, I was very fortunate to have the full support of many members of the Providence Creek Academy former staff, including Chuck Taylor, who had been one of the founding board members that took possession of the abandoned school in the late 1990's. From the moment the PCA members took possession of the property it became apparent that within the buildings not everything was quite normal, and that echoes of the past might be resonating into the future.

"We started the foundation around 2000 or thereabouts. There was another gentleman and I, Jim G., and I." The two men arranged for the transfer of the property from the Josephites in 1999, but it wasn't until 2000 that Chuck and Jim began the reconstruction of the buildings.

He recalls taking a tour of the buildings before purchasing the property. He noted that the newly named Morrell Hall was the building where the Priests and nuns had resided, before decamping. Apparently when the church called them home, they left the building intact. "It was like you left your home, turned the key and never returned. There were dishes on the table, beds were still made. It was just amazing how they left one day, locked the door, and never came back. "

"We tried to solicit groups to give money to help with the revival of the property." What this entailed were many fund-raising events in the gym to garner support from the local constabulary. "So, we had different groups come in, and it was at one of these events when I had my first experience." They were running a talent show among students from Clayton and Smyrna one Saturday afternoon, and the students were performing on the stage to the back of the gym.

"The gym was the only space that was really open." The two wings of the school building were closed off awaiting construction. They had once been the dorms of St. Joseph's "A and B-wings and C and D-wings were closed and there was no one down there because it was all original. They had been used as dorms, and they still had the bathrooms and shower rooms that the boys had used on each of the wings."

Chuck recalled a bizarre fund-raising event being held in the gymnasium. They had a group of students performing on the stage. The whole event was being broadcast via a PA system.

"So, we had a group performing and they were using a PA system and microphones for the singers. And suddenly the PA system just stopped for no reason." The kids that were singing stopped singing, supposedly when they realized the PA system was down.

Chuck the recalled, "And out of nowhere we all heard the sound of a vacuum cleaner." It sounded like an industrial vacuum cleaner.

Chuck was aware of the sound, but apparently didn't think too much of it, being more concerned with getting the PA system back up and functioning. To that end he headed toward the front of the gym toward the door. As he approached the door to the gym, he noticed a group of around five or six people outside the door to the gymnasium huddled together in the Main Hall and looking down C-wing, which was closed with a door that had a pane of glass.

Through the pane of glass on a locked door of an abandoned hall, through another door and window into what had been a dorm room, everyone gazed upon an odd sight. They all could clearly see a gentleman at the very end of C-Wing…vacuuming.

"It was a person, but it wasn't a person, if you know what I mean. There was no access to that area, because C-Wing was closed off, completely." Everyone in the group was confused as to the identity of the man. "They were all asking each other, 'Hey who is that guy and how did he get in there?' We never saw his face, just the back and side of his face and his arms moving as if he was pushing a vacuum cleaner."

Chuck noted that everyone in the group could see the man, and that they all got the chills, knowing innately that what they were witnessing was otherworldly. The man was wearing casual clothing, such as a custodian would wear. Chuck thought he recalled bib overalls of a jean material. He also recalled that the man was an older man of around his fifties or sixties. Because Chuck couldn't see a face clearly, he couldn't identify the race of the man. As the group gazed at the gentleman, he remained leaned forward with his arm moving as if he was hard at work vacuuming a rug. As construction had not yet started, there was still no electrical power in C-Wing, and none of the lights were working. So even if a rogue custodian managed to break into the building hell bent on cleaning, he wouldn't have been able to power his vacuum.

A few seconds later the music came back on and everything went back to normal. The group dispersed back to the talent show.

Chuck and another man, obviously concerned that there was someone on C-Wing, unlocked the door and headed down to find the interloper. By then the phantom custodian was completely gone. They found absolutely nothing in C-wing but the debris of past echoes.

Contractors Harassed

There were asbestos workers in the building removing ceiling tiles and old flooring tiles that were riddled with the substance. Chuck was on the property one day, checking on the progress of the workers, when the foreman approached him. He told Chuck that one of his crew had just walked off the job. The crew member had been working on C-Wing, when he saw "someone." The man quit that day and left the property quickly. It wouldn't be the only contractor over the years to leave abruptly. They would report seeing apparitions, hearing footsteps, and hearing voices, where no one could possibly be.

Children Spirits

To fund the project, Chuck worked closely with a local bank. When the asbestos was fully removed and it was finally safe, Chuck had a small group of bankers in to view the property one day. They were examining the construction on C-Wing as Chuck elaborated on the school's plans. The whole group was standing in what would become one of PCA's classrooms. Each wing was divided up into six classrooms and each classroom had a door that led out to a narrow courtyard. Originally A and C-Wing had been the Boy's Dormitory Wings.

As Chuck was addressing the group, with his face to the back door, he noticed movement outside. He saw what he thought was a boy of 12 or 13 years of age, an extremely interesting fact as St. Joseph's had been a middle school, and the students would have been that age.

"The boy looked startled when he realized I was looking at him. He was either Caucasian or Native American." St Joseph's had admitted Native American boys at the school as well.

The boy was running or walking briskly from the gym area toward the center of the long narrow courtyard, right towards Chuck and the bankers. In between the classroom Chuck was in and the rear door to the gym was another access door and the door and steps to the basement. Just then one of the bankers asked Chuck a question, and Chuck turned his gaze away from the window to the banker.

"I turned back not longer than a couple of seconds later and there's no one there. "

Chuck immediately exited the classroom door into the courtyard to find the child. Having not run past them, there were only a couple of alternatives; the boy must have entered the building by either the service door or basement door which were both boarded up and locked. Wherever the child went hadn't been into the building.

Out in the narrow courtyard, Chuck quickly realized that the boy hadn't escaped his notice by natural means. All the windows and doors were still boarded up from the building's long years of vacancy.

"The doors and windows were completely boarded up." He tried the boards to make sure they were still secured. They were. The only other explanation was that the boy had climbed a ladder to the roof. Chuck checked for ladders and found none.

"There was no place for this kid to go, zero, and he disappeared just like that. There was absolutely nowhere the boy could have gone that I wouldn't have been able to see him, and somehow, he'd simply disappeared, which was the weirdest part. And that was my second encounter."

The lad had been wearing jeans and a t-shirt or shirt, nondescript in other words. His clothing and demeanor had been so natural that his sudden disappearance left Chuck at a loss for a rational explanation.

Caretaker Encounters

Chuck noted that the school buildings had literally been built on top of an underground stream that snakes all the way across the property. Hence the basements were always a point of concern. If a sump pump failed, the basements would flood. So, they had the property caretaker periodically check the pumps in the basements of Drexel and St. Michael's. The caretaker, doing his nightly rounds, was in the basement of Drexel right around 7:00 or 8:00 in the evening, checking on the pump. Pump checked, the caretaker turned around and realized he wasn't alone. There was a figure of a man standing right behind him. He relayed the incident to Chuck.

By then, it appears, Chuck was the recipient of many stories. Frequently teachers and custodial staff would tell him about phantom sounds they heard, and lights turning on and off. Those, especially employees who came in early or stayed late into the evening, had experiences. Strange noises were frequent. Sometimes he'd hear of even stranger things. A teacher would leave, turn off the lights, lock the door of a classroom and come back the next morning to find the room rearranged. Most of the odd events occurred on C-Wing.

"C-Wing and the basement, that was where most of the activity happened."

Chuck remains friendly with one of the school's former kindergarten teachers. She recalls a day when she left her classroom on A-wing to use the ladies' room. She entered the room and knew immediately that there was someone in the room with her.

"She said the hair on her arms stood up, and she had that weird feeling that someone was there watching her. She told me she's never vacated a room so quickly in her life.

When someone is present, even when that person cannot be seen, they can be sensed. The electrical-static response our bodies give off is an indicator that someone else is around. And while cliché, the hair on the back of the neck standing up is a good indicator that you are not alone, especially if you were otherwise on a normal daily routine.

I'm a proponent of trusting those instincts as real, even if not verified. In my family, we refer to those events as iron bracelet events. Several years ago, I had several iron bracelets made by a blacksmith. They're decorative, in that they're decorated in Gaelic designs, but they also serve as protection against the other side.

I tend to adhere to the old beliefs that iron is a deterrent to paranormal entities. Older generations had to deal with paranormal activity with no scientific advances whatsoever. They found that iron had a tendency to dampen paranormal activity. Hence the old belief that to kill a vampire you had to pound an iron nail into their heart. I don't know if vampires really exist. I doubt not, but I believe they're a more anamorphous drain on our energy. I do know, after years of investigating, that activity tends to follow me home. When you look at paranormal activity, it tends to look back. From my family's perspective, when we see an uptick in odd events, we throw on the iron bracelets, and we have a quiet night's sleep. You don't have to believe, or disbelieve. If we don an iron bracelet, we're not plagued by nightmares or late-night visitations.

While activity has been reported all over the property, Chuck adamantly stated that it was C-Wing that was the most active. C-Wing was where the phantom custodian vacuumed to an audience, and where the boy was seen through a window, and then remarkably vanished only seconds later.

I would quickly be led to concur, hearing the reports of other employees.

Chuck continued, "Something happened on C-Wing, something *happened* on C-Wing, that's where all this originates from. I was in that building at all hours of the day and night when we were developing the school. I'd be checking on things, making sure the sump pump was working and we weren't flooding the basement. I'd be in the other buildings, and…there was something there. I'd swear on a stack of bibles to that fact." C-Wing's reputation for paranormal activity would continue when the next owners took possession as well, but it should be said, the paranormal activity continues all over the grounds of St. Joseph's.

Providence Creek Academy remained in the buildings until 2007, when the foundation built a larger, all- purpose school building to accommodate their growing student population.

Mr. Vaughn was the groundskeeper/custodian that lived on the property when it was vacant and remained through the PCA years. Many of those I spoke with recalled Mr. Vaughn fondly. He appeared to be a stoic individual, a quiet presence of calm when needed.

The cemetery, in a wooded area to the back of the property, became the burial ground for priests and brothers that passed away. It also served as a cemetery for the St. Polycarp parishioners that also shared the Chapel for local services. Chuck believes that there were also a couple of unmarked graves where a boy or two were perhaps buried.

There is a rumor that someone had been buried beneath the large statue at the front entrance to the school property. Chuck admitted that they'd had the property placed on the Historical Registry so that the buildings and grounds could be preserved as they stand now.

He admitted that the most activity was reported in the two years when the property was under renovation. That is typical of paranormal activity. Twenty some years of calm and peace and then strangers come in swinging hammers and tearing out walls usually garner an uptick in interest from the other side.

Leah,
Former Student of Providence Creek Academy

Leah, a former student at Providence Creek Academy, is now an English teacher in Japan. She left PCA in 2013. Shen went through the switching of the school from the old buildings to the new building when she was in fifth grade. She remembers the old brick buildings, and the Chapel in particular.

"I remember that church. I remember that church so vividly. I don't know if it was just me being a kid and over imagining it now. But I spent a lot of time in that church." PCA had used the Chapel for their music and dance programs. Leah had been in the ballet program, and that's where they practiced until the Chapel had to be shut down. The walls of the old Chapel have become the home of wasps and bees. The wasps have literally burrowed into the wood and walls of the old structure. Thus, no matter how many cans of bug killer the teachers sprayed, the Chapel was always full of stinging insects in the spring and summer months, making it very dangerous for the children. There's also no plumbing in the Chapel, meaning that every trip to the bathroom required a hike across the campus grounds. Sadly, while the Chapel is a lovely, architectural gem, functionally it's a nightmare.

Leah said that she's a ghost detractor, and although she knew students who had experienced phenomena in the Chapel, she never actually experienced anything. She remembers specifically hearing accounts of hearing children running around in the Choir Loft. None of the students were actually allowed into the Choir Loft, as the stairs were deemed not structurally sound. To keep the students safe, the staff strictly forbid anyone from going up into the loft. So, if a child had been up running in the loft, they would have been breaking the rules and were lying.

"I do remember looking up at that loft and thinking it would be creepy if someone was up there. I'm not going to think about that anymore, because I'm seven. I do remember my teacher stopping and looking up at the loft, as if she'd seen something move up there. She just kind of paused and stared up there with a puzzled look like, 'well I don't know what that was.' But we didn't care and so she just went on like nothing was the matter. Any time we heard anything in the Chapel, we just assumed it was the bees, because the place was infected with bees and wasps. I just remember the colors, the off-white, and the greenish blue color that everything was painted in and the buzzing of the bees. "

Leah was one of the younger kids in the group, and recalls that the older girls would often tell tales to scare the younger. There were two girls, a grade ahead of Leah, who would arrive at the Chapel first to set up for ballet training. They would arrive to move the pews and the chairs out of the way to open the space for the dancers. "I remember them saying they arrived one day and that they were talking and doing a little dancing, playing the ballet music, and waiting for the rest of the group to arrive. Suddenly the two girls heard something fall." They assumed it had been one of the chairs that they had stacked to make room for the dancers. "So, they were worried, assuming that one of the chairs that they had stacked had broken. But the chairs were fine.

So, then they wondered, 'well where did that sound come from?'" So, then they looked up at the Choir Loft and a box in the Loft had fallen over. Being forbidden to go up there, they just stood and looked toward the loft, rather unnerved. Obviously, a sound so loud they assumed it to be a broken chair must have resounded through the building eerily.

"After that day they used the tale to scare us. 'Ewww, there's a ghost up there, we heard them.' But they had been generally freaked out when it happened. I remember they would whisper about it amongst themselves, instead of gloating about it to the younger students."

The lights in the Chapel would flicker on and off, but the students figured it was an old building with old wiring. The lights in the corners of the altar area in particular would flicker often. "We assumed that there were bees and wasps in the walls. Who's to say they weren't nibbling at the wiring? So, it was hard to take any ghost related stories about the building seriously. It was so old, and it had kind of a creepy vibe. So, every time someone would say, 'oh, there's a ghost here,' we would say, 'so what of it. Dah, it's a creepy, old church. What can we do about it.'" While it was delightfully interesting to have a resident spirit or spirits, in the same vein, the girls really didn't want to experience them.

The basement of Drexel was an area that was especially creepy. During the interview, Leah asked me pointedly whether the team had gone down there. I told her that we had. The basement of Drexel was where the custodian had been checking the sump pump and encountered the dark figure standing behind him. The basement was definitely on our radar that night.

Then she asked me something that took me completely by surprise. She asked, "Does it still look like a perfectly preserved 1940's classroom?" I was stymied by the question, because the basement is now a very damp exercise room, full of exercise machines, free weights, and weight benches for the athletes to use.

"Oh! When I was there, we had a tornado warning one afternoon. It was after school and we were practicing our ballet." The teacher called a halt to practice and trooped her charges down to the basement to wait out the storm. Leah had never been in the basement, and she was in for a shock.

"I kid you not, it was a perfectly preserved 1940's 1950's style [classroom], black blackboard, and chalk style classroom. All of the desks were perfectly aligned in neat rows. There were still papers and pencils on the desks. There was writing on the chalkboard. I wish I'd taken some of the papers, out of curiosity, but I was eight and afraid of the possibility of a tornado. There was a single bulb hanging from the ceiling, the 'click on clicks off, creepy murder basement sort of light.' It was as if the people had just left. And I just stood there and wondered, 'Why was it all still there?'"

"Apparently no one used this basement for anything. It was just so strange, because it was perfect. And I think that freaked me out more than anything. My mother was there, because she'd come to pick me up. We'd gone down to the basement with the rest of the group. We still talk about that basement to this day. There wasn't another chalkboard anywhere at the school at that point. We had only white boards. And the desks weren't wooden anymore; we had only metal desks. Why, if they had gotten rid of everything else, had they left this room untouched? It was just so eerie. It was like we'd stepped back to 1953, but all the people had disappeared. It was like a perfect time capsule, and it was so weird."

"I remember the classroom in the basement and the church as being these weird, eerie, moments of my childhood. And I don't really know how to explain it to anyone. Something just felt so wrong about those places, and yet it was oddly, sickeningly fascinating at the same time."

Lauren,
Former Providence Creek Academy Teacher

Lauren was a former teacher at PCA. She has since left the state, but her first years of teaching were at PCA. She recalled a number of experiences that even though several years have now gone by, still remain quite vivid in her memory.

"I worked at Providence Creek Academy for seven years, from December of 2003 until December of 2010. I have several stories about Providence Creek Academy. Let's start in the Chapel. I used to teach dance in the Chapel, so when we first started the dance program we used the Chapel, which was great because it had bees everywhere, and we had small children and no bathroom. What better area for five-year-olds, right?" One night with the rest of the school shut down, the dance teachers and their young charges had just finished a dance practice. Parents were arriving to take the children home, waiting for them in the vestibule.

There is a small vestibule area when you first enter the Chapel. On either side of the vestibule are dual stairs that lead up to the choir loft. To enter the Chapel itself, you have to pass through another set of doors.

"It was the end of class, and the kids were getting dressed in the Chapel, so they didn't have to leave school in their leotards and tights. I stepped into the vestibule area, to talk to the parents about an upcoming event we had planned. There were several parents, and the dancers were slowly coming into the vestibule as they finished changing. I was talking with the parents, when I noticed that I was hearing the sounds of children running around.

The children started to trickle through from the Chapel. So now I had most of the children present in the vestibule. I looked around and started to say, 'Who on Earth would let their children go upstairs and play in the Choir Loft?' But then I looked around and realized that none of the parents had children young enough to be doing that. So, we all stopped and looked upwards, because there were the definite sounds of children playing overhead.

There was the sound of footsteps of a child running around in the choir loft, and no one else was in the building. By the time I'd spoken that statement, all the children had come through to the vestibule. There were five or six parents, and five or six kids. I had just finished my spiel."

Having finished disseminating her information, she realized that the noises of children upstairs were still evident. "We all just stopped and looked around, and then everyone became very quiet."

"There was definitely someone up there. You could hear the sound of laughing, playing and the feet running back and forth. That's why I thought it was children. That's why it was my first teacher's instinct to say what I did. But there was nobody up there. Everyone heard it." Eventually the sounds just stopped, and no child or children ever came down the Choir Loft stairs.

Lauren taught kindergarten for seven years. Her classroom was situated on A-Wing of Drexel Hall, which, while not as notorious as C-Wing, has had its own share of stories over the years. At the time, Lauren was a first-year teacher, which is an excruciatingly busy year for an educator, as you're creating everything you're using in class, as well as teaching and grading. Lauren was also overseeing the ballet troupe. She would be with the ballet students until 6:00 to 6:30 every evening, returning to her classroom after that to set up and prepare for the next day's classes. The workload was such that she often stayed at school late into the evening preparing for the next day before calling it a night.

"School would end at 3:45pm, but I would be in my classroom working until seven or eight in the evenings, and some nights it was even later than that. Vaughn, the caretaker, became my very best friend on those nights, because he was always there." She became friendly with Mr. Vaughn, who often stopped by for a chat while on his rounds. She was single at the time, alone late at night in a mostly empty building. A friendly face and a conversation with an adult would have been a welcome relief.

Vaughn, the property's caretaker, lived in the small apartment on the other side of the art building. He'd been the caretaker through the years when St. Joseph's had stood vacant, and he remained when Providence Creek Academy took over the property as well. He mowed the grass and served as security, walking the grounds and buildings at night.

For the ballet classes, Lauren got a disc player that ran off batteries. Outlets were scarce in the Chapel, and it had no dedicated sound system, so Lauren used the battery-operated radio to play the ballet music for her young charges. This night, she had the radio playing in her classroom. She'd placed the music player in the center of the room on a desk, and was playing music from a CD using the batteries.

She was working at her desk, listening to the music, when the school underwent a short black out. All the lights and electronics in the building just suddenly turned off and a few seconds later came back up. What was odd about the event was that the CD player stopped working as well, when the lights went down, and then came back on when the lights came up, playing at the same spot on the CD that it had been playing before. She didn't think anything of it until she remembered that the radio wasn't plugged in. "I didn't think a whole lot about it, and then I turned and realized that the radio was in the center of the room, and there's no plug. So, whatever turned the lights off also turned the radio off, and then back on."

But the episode that really unnerved Lauren happened again very late at night in a nearly abandoned building. Lauren was working in her classroom. Vaughn had stopped by to say hello and was somewhere on the property doing his rounds. There was also a male and female janitor cleaning in two separate halls. She didn't know them by name; she just knew they were fairly new to the positions. Lauren recalls that the night time janitorial staff turned over frequently at PCA, and I suspect I know the reason for the frequent turnover.

"So, they were cleaning Drexel Hall and I was in my classroom. Now the PA system in the building ran through the phones." The PA system could also reach any other building on the property as well. Announcements were made in the school office, which is right off the main entrance of Drexel Hall. The Main Office had windows running along the entire front of the office and the one wall opposite the Main Hall. From the main hallway that runs the entire length of the school building, the Main Office is quite visible, and anyone in the Main Office would also be starkly visible as well.

There was an announcement that came through the PA system that evening. It was a woman's voice and she was in distress. She asked if anyone was there and asked for help. "I ran out of my classroom on A-Wing thinking it must be the woman who was cleaning. As I came down the main hall, the female janitor emerged from C-Wing thinking it must have been me who had made the announcement. Then the male janitor emerged from D-Wing (the furthest wing of the building from the Front entrance), to make sure we were all right."

"So, we're all three standing in the middle of the hall, asking each other, 'Was it you? Was it you?' And, of course, it wasn't any of us. We had no plausible explanation as to where the help call came from." Where they converged, the three would have had a clear shot of the Main Office, which was dark, locked up tight for the evening.

"Now there may have been an all-call code for the PA system that would allow you to make a PA announcement from a phone anywhere. But I didn't know what the code was. They didn't publicize the code. And the kicker was there was no one else on the property that night. Ours were the only three cars in the parking lot. We were the only three people in the building." She remembers that there were no lights visible in Morrell Hall, which housed many of the school's administrative offices.

"I'm not sure anyone ever figured out where the call originated. I talked to Chuck, the managing director, and Audrey, the principal, the next day. I told them, 'This happened last night and we couldn't account for it. They told me no one was there. It wasn't a Board Meeting Night." Morrell Hall, she reiterated, had no visible lights on in the building.

"After that, I packed up my things and went home that night. I was done." The janitors had to stay, but they elected to stay together instead of separating in different wings. As she departed the building she would have gone right by the Main Office. All the lights were off, the door locked. Clearly no one living had made the call for help in a nearly empty building.

"Things would happen there at night. I felt comfortable in my room at night, but I wasn't going to venture out into the rest of the school because it was just eerie."

Lauren recalled the tornado warning that sent them all to the basement of Drexel. She had everyone crawl into the tunnel underneath the school, deeming it the safest spot. It was a weird place, that tunnel, as the ceiling was low and the tunnel was dusty and dirty from disuse. "It was just creepy, though nothing happened."

"What happened to me at that school made me a believer, and I don't typically believe in that kind of stuff. And it doesn't align with my religious beliefs *at all*." Whenever anything in the building happened, it was typically quite late in the evening, around eight at night, when everyone else but the janitorial staff and perhaps one over-burdened, first-year elementary teacher labored on in the quiet, empty rooms.

Audrey Erschen,
Former Principal, Providence Creek Academy

Audrey started her 17-year tenure at Providence Creek Academy as a Special Education teacher. Eventually she assumed the duties of principal and moved into what is now the Commandant's Office in Drexel Hall – the office directly across from the windowed Main School Office. The main doorway area led out again to the long main hall that runs the entire length of the building.

Obviously, the duties of being principal often resulted in long hours in her office, when all the children and teachers went home. Nearly every night she stayed late, she recalls hearing unaccountable sounds in the main entryway or hall region of the school. She would hear footsteps in empty parts of the building, doors opening and closing. Once a disembodied giggle that seemed to come out of nowhere. "It was like they were having a good time, and they were laughing." Occasionally, she heard the sounds of a basketball from the gymnasium, as if someone was playing a game of hoops. Lights would flicker. "If I was there by myself, every time I was there alone, I would hear something." These occurred so frequently that she became attuned to them, thinking of them as just the natural sounds of an old building.

But one evening she distinctly heard music, old music, like a waltz. The music was so oddly out of place that it drew her from her office.

"One evening I heard music, and I thought well, I must have a teacher in the building." She ignored the music for a while, as it wasn't loud. While low, she did notice that the music was from a bygone era, which eventually sparked her interest. Finally, out of curiosity, she decided to follow the music to find its source. "So, I walked towards C-wing. I didn't see any lights on, but I continued to hear the music." As she turned and looked down C-Wing, she saw a wonderment that she never could have expected.

"As I turned to look down the C-Wing hallway there was a couple…dancing in the hallway." She couldn't believe what she was seeing, and she started to look around to see if she was the only one witnessing the sight. "And I turned and looked back down the main hallway, and it was just me, and I turned back, and there they were dancing as if they were at a party or a dance."

It wasn't just that there were two people dancing in C-Wing, it was that this couple was quite obviously out of time. She was dressed in an old-fashioned "settlers" gown which looked to be cotton. He was in an unremarkable dark suit with a longer jacket, solid in color. When I asked if the man might have been a priest or a brother, Audrey said no, he was just a young man enjoying the company of a lady.

Upon questioning Audrey, she thought the music was a waltz. She noted that the music seemed to be recorded and played as if from a record on an old gramophone. There were scratches and pops, as if being played on an older, much used recording.

Audrey knew, from past reports of the activity in the school, that what she was seeing wasn't real. "I made that assumption, because I'd been at the school when it opened, and several others had recalled stories of seeing ghosts and the place being haunted. So, I assumed what I was seeing was paranormal. But I wasn't afraid. If anything, it was a very peaceful scene. Yes, I did get chills, but I wasn't afraid."

The dancers were young. Audrey estimated them to be in their mid to late twenties. The dark-haired youth held his lady love close, so close that Audrey never got a good look at the lovers' faces.

Audrey estimated the woman's dress to be from the early nineteenth century. When I sent her several pictures of dresses and had her identify the one that was closest to the dress the woman was wearing, Audrey chose a type of calico, everyday dress popular in the 1840's to 1860s', with a fitted bodice and a larger skirt. From studying the different dress patterns, the larger bell-shaped skirts were ubiquitous in the mid-1800's when hoop skirts and petticoats were worn to enlarge the bell shape. The dress might be later in the 1800's, however, after the 1860's skirt fashions tended to get even wider. In the early 20th century skirt styles reversed, becoming narrower and eventually shorter.

The man's longer suit jacket fits with the same time period of the mid 1800's, when jackets typically got longer, sometimes as long as the top of the knee.

The idea that the music was from a record doesn't appear to fit with this time frame, however. While Edison invented the Victrola in 1877, sales of the device were lackluster. Wide distribution of the gramophone didn't actually occur until the turn of the 20th century.

She recalls that the couple seemed to be right out of an old movie. "They were grainy, though they did appear solid." There were definite shapes, although I couldn't make out facial features. I could clearly see the outline of her dress, and his arm as he held her tight."

"And they were having a grand time. I didn't feel afraid, because the couple seemed completely oblivious to anyone but themselves."

Audrey stood transfixed in the hallway, she knows not how long, watching the wistful dancers. The song finally ended. At one point, Audrey came out of her reverie. She turned her head for a moment and then turned back, and the dancers were gone. "The song faded out and they were done showing me that they were there was the impression I got at the time." The dancers had faded back to the past with the last plaintive notes of the violins.

The second remarkable experience Audrey had occurred in the morning, again on the infamous C-Wing. She had arrived early to open the school, unlocking classroom doors, and turning on lights. "I don't know if it was a shadow that moved or I caught movement out of the corner of my eye." When she looked out the classroom window, she saw a child. She reports that it appeared to be a small child of three and a half to four feet, with shoulder length, curly, blond-hair. She recalls that the child seemed to be wearing a beige colored tunic top. She couldn't see the legs of the child as they were below the sills of the windows. She described the tunic as simple in design, something like medical scrubs. She never saw the child's face as their head was in profile, and she couldn't be sure of the gender.

The child was between C-Wing and the gym, in the narrow courtyard area, where Chuck had seen the boy. Audrey assumed one of the students had arrived at school early. She witnessed the child running past the windows of the classroom, and, when she went to the next classroom, saw them run past that set of windows as well.

The child was so lifelike it never occurred to Audrey that she wasn't seeing one of the P.C.A. students. "And the child was out there running around playing peek-a-boo with me as I was opening up the classrooms. The scene was in color, and the child appeared human…real. I thought one of the kids had come to school early, looking for a way in and saw me flipping on lights, and was trying to get my attention."

Audrey went out the back door of the classroom to let the child into the building. "And when I walked out the door there was no one to be seen. I walked around the little courtyard area between the two buildings. I checked the steps going down into the basement outside, I wandered back around the school and I didn't see anyone. But I know what I saw. I saw a blond-haired child run past two sets of classroom windows and then vanish."

Audrey's son reported on the same call that often when he was in the basement of Morrell Hall, the water would often turn on by itself, an activity often reported in Drexel as well. They seem to have an affinity for the plumbing, but then ghosts don't have to pay the water bills.

As the principal, she spoke with other teachers, and they would relate incidents that had happened to them. The choir director who held rehearsals in the Chapel noted that sometimes when he was holding practice a voice would join the group of singers that was otherworldly.

Audrey retired in 2019, and was there when the First State Military Academy founders took over the building. She did say that she never felt threatened by the activity at the school.

"It was always playful; it wasn't malicious. I was never fearful of being there alone whether at night or during the day. I never felt like I was alone, but I was never afraid."

Jessica,
Former PCA student

A senior in college now, Jessica was in fifth grade the last year that PCA inhabited the old campus buildings. Her mother was also a teacher at PCA. Jessica said, "Everyone that went to school there had creepy feelings. You felt like you were never alone," a sentiment which mirrors Audrey's observation exactly. She went on to comment that she often felt watched while she was there.

Jessica's personal experience occurred in the Chapel. She was there for a music enrichment class one day. All the students were lined up to leave at the end of it. As they began to march out, Jessica was inclined to look up at the ceiling. "I don't know why, but I just had an instinct to look up."

There was a ceiling tile out, and looking down through the gap in the tile was a strange set of eyes gazing at her. "I vividly remember it; I could draw a picture of it. It's just that putting it into words is difficult. The eyes were red and glowing, but they weren't the neon red glowing eyes you see depicted in movies." These eyes were a maroon red, and everything else around them, "was just a black missing hole in the ceiling." She only had a few moments to observe the eyes, before the teacher told the students they had to leave for the next class. She isn't sure if she was the only one that saw the eyes or if other children saw them as well and just didn't say anything about them. "Being in fifth grade, I really didn't know how to react. I just went about my day, thinking 'that was weird.'"

Jessica's mother had a co-worker who was part of the ballet dance troupe. She related this story to Jessica's mother, who related it to Jessica. The instructor noted that they had held a dance recital in the Chapel one evening. The dance recital over, all the students and parents had left, and the two teachers were getting ready to lock up for the night.

Suddenly they heard the sounds of, "what sounded like ten kids" running in circles in the Choir Loft above their heads. They had thought they were the only ones in the building and had been about to leave. Obviously, they couldn't lock up a building if there were children still in it. One teacher stayed on the ground floor by the door and the stairs in the vestibule, and one teacher started climbing the stairs to the Choir Loft.

When she hit the top step, the sounds of running feet ceased. In the sudden stillness she found no children. The teacher that remained on the first floor confirmed that no children had come down the other set of stairs when the teacher was ascending. They searched the building and found no one. They were utterly alone. Jessica said that she'd confirmed the details of the story with her mother before doing the interview with me.

She concluded that the old campus is "notorious for being haunted. Everyone who went to PCA and even the residents of Clayton or Smyrna knows it."

Beverly Eaton,
Parent of P.C.A. student

Beverly's son attended Providence Creek Academy. When he was in kindergarten the school put on an outdoor Halloween parade. The Chapel was unlocked that day, and Beverly's mother and step-father had decided to take a peek around the otherwise closed off building. The Chapel has that effect on people as the lovely yet abandoned building lures through mystery.

The two had entered to take a clandestine look around. Beverly had asked her mom, while she was inside, to take a few pictures of the glorious stained-glass windows that adorn the Chapel from floor to ceiling. When developed, the pictures showed white blobs that oddly didn't appear on the negatives.

More disturbing yet was a picture to the right of the foyer doorway of what appeared to be a little girl. The image apparently was so distinct that mother and daughter thought they could see the child's dark hair and dress. Beverly described the dress as looking dated. The color of the garment was a beige or a brown, possibly patterned with long sleeves.

She was only visible from the waist up, so the length of the garment was not discernible. The hair was brown and long with a side part. The hair looked disheveled, stringy, and snarled, according to Beverly, as if it hadn't been brushed for a long while. The figure appeared to be crouched down by the stained-glass window, and in the image, she appeared to be screaming.

"It was like she was scared, and she was crouched down. She had both hands covering her ears, and her elbows were sticking out. Her mouth was wide open, as if she was screaming." The girl was semi-translucent, with the wall being visible behind her.

There was, of course, no one in the Chapel; all the children were outside. The image of the strange child also appeared on the negative as well. Beverly's mother didn't see the child with her own eyes; it was only on reviewing the photos that the image was noticed. Thinking it might be a double negative, Beverly looked at the whole roll of pictures. All of the children present that day had been in costume, and there were no children that were in that particular pose, or looked like the child in the photograph. Unfortunately, Beverly couldn't find the photographs at the time of the interview.

Beverly then recounted another experience she had, not at the school but at Fort Delaware, another spot that the team had investigated. It turns out Beverly had the great opportunity of seeing the elusive female cook in the officer's kitchen. The Fort staff were doing one of their frequent re-enactments that day. Beverly and her son, who was an infant at the time, were watching the performers from the kitchen. The child was heavy, so Beverly was holding him to the back of the group. Out in the cobbled courtyard area, Beverly could hear footsteps approaching.

When she looked behind her, standing in the doorway of the kitchen was an African American woman in period dress. She was wearing a blue pastel calico dress with a white apron over the top. She also sported a white kerchief over her hair. Beverly was impressed with the amount of preparation that had gone into the reenactment, right down to the singed hem of the woman's long dress, a detail I have read from other accounts of the same female apparition.

"I thought they'd really thought about all of the details. I could physically see her as I was standing there. I just thought she was another actress there as part of the demonstration."

Beverly turned and looked at the woman, who acknowledged her presence by looking over at her. She then turned her gaze away from Beverly and looked down, towards the ground.

"Then she literally turned around and walked through the door. The door was closed. She actually walked *through* the door."

Some of the people on the tour also reported seeing the woman standing in the doorway, although Beverly didn't admit to it at the time. It wasn't until she read a book about the hauntings at the Fort that she realized whom she had seen. The author had described the same African-American cook and gave her the name of Sophia.

Also, that same day the Fort had scheduled the firing of a live cannon. There was a schedule for the firings. Beverly was upstairs on the battlement when she distinctly heard the boom of a cannon being fired. The curious thing about the boom was it was an hour and a half before the firing was scheduled. Hearing the firing of the cannon prompted her to look at the schedule, thinking they'd missed the event. There were two other adults on the battlements at the time, who also heard the booming fire. The booming of a ghostly cannon was something the team experienced on our investigation of the Fort as well, so it serves as a curious coincidence.

Chapel at night

Chapter Three:

Police Get Involved

Scott Harvey,
Police Officer, Clayton Police Department

It seems that the spirits that played with the electrical systems weren't always satisfied to only play their games during daylight hours, but would often continue their pranks into the wee hours of the night, when it came under the purview of the local police department.

An officer of the Clayton Police Department, Scott Harvey, related to me his long and mysterious association with both the school and the grounds that started when he was a young man in the Marine Corps and continued when he became an officer on the local force.

As a rookie officer, Scott often worked the night shift for the Clayton force, and hence was called in on several occasions at the school, usually when alarm systems would seemingly malfunction. The police got called on just one such night, when the rookie cop was on night duty. Scott and his former partner responded to an alarm in Drexel Hall, indicating a possible break in.

The two were checking doors on the side of the building where A-Wing is located, and found one that was oddly left unlocked. They headed down the main hallway that runs the entire length of the building, past the cafeteria and the gym and eventually arrived at the turn off to C-Wing hallway. Both noticed that they were hearing scratching noises on a window at the end of the hall. It sounded, according to Scott, to be very much like a tree branch brushing up against a window. Both officers distinctly heard the noises but didn't think too much about it, as it was rather a mundane sound, except that it continued as they approached the end of the hall.

They determined that the window where the scratching sound came was either a window next to the emergency door or the window on the emergency door itself. When it didn't abate, the two formed a plan to determine the source of the scratching. Scott's partner told him that he'd stay inside, and Scott should exit the building from the door they had entered, and walk around the back of the building to see if they figure out whether the scratching was of vegetative origin or being done by a human interloper. As Scott headed back out, they were in contact through their radios. Scott's partner continued to report that he was still hearing the scraping noises.

Meanwhile Scott had walked back down the main hallway and departed the building from the door they had entered. He walked around the rear of the building to where his partner was waiting. As he approached the area, he could still distinctly hear the scratching as well. But when he arrived, Scott didn't find the tree or bush that he had expected to be there. Indeed, there was no vegetation at all near the door or the back of the building. Of course, just as he reached his destination the scratching instantly ceased. Neither man could hear a thing. A search of the building revealed no one was there. They didn't know why one of the doors was unlocked and never determined what had set off the alarm in the first place. The two, now rather confused, police officers left the building quickly after that.

A second episode occurred at the school one night when Scott had an intern doing a ride along with him. The two got called to the Chapel for an alarm at around 2:00 a.m. The two circled the Chapel checking to make sure the doors were locked, when they detected the sound of a child laughing. As the pair were trying doors, which were locked as they should have been, they could find no discernible reason for the alarm on the inside of the church to have sounded.

But the sounds of the laughing child started to pique their interest. The laughter seemed to be emanating from outside the building not within, and the laughter also seemed to be playing a joke on the two officers. If they were on one side of the building, they would hear laughing on the other side of the structure. They'd circle around to find that now the laughing was coming from the side they had just left. Scott admitted that the event was more eerie than the unidentifiable scratching noises they'd encountered in C-Wing of Drexel Hall. Still, if there was a child outside playing at this early morning time, the officers wanted to find her or him, thinking the child might be lost.

They decided to split up, to foil the child in their game of cat and mouse. When they were on opposite sides of the building, the laughter ceased. But when they regrouped, the laughing would commence, always on the side of the building that they had just vacated, but the sounds were clear and distinct, and they thought they'd turn a corner at any time and find a child of around five or six years old pranking them.

Scott admitted the two performed their due diligence looking for the lost child, circling the Chapel and the grounds for 45 minutes or more. They finally had to give up the hunt, chalking it up to just one more creepy occurrence at St. Joe's. He admitted they never have been able to determine what set off the alarms, though he was called out to the school on numerous occasions.

Scott recounted a bizarre call from a resident of the area, who claimed that there was toxic waste buried on the grounds of the school by the pond. Scott and his partner responded to the call which came in at night, as luck would have it. They were traipsing the grounds around the wooded pond, some distance from the school, when both of their flashlights drained of power. He said they could see them getting dimmer, and then dimmer, before they both stopped functioning. This was confusing as it is not the way that the flashlights normally function.

He noted that they were rechargeable flashlights with a working charge of 12 hours or more - enough power to last an entire shift if necessary. When not in use the flashlights are on charging bases within their squad car. Still, both stopped working, leaving the two men shambling around in the dark woods in confusion. Both believed that their flashlights had been fully charged before setting off.

They never found the said toxic waste, and Scott didn't even recall who the strange caller had been. They didn't see or hear anything particularly frightening as they walked carefully out of the woods and back to their vehicle. They just couldn't account for how both flashlights could have been completely drained at the same time.

One evening, as Providence Creek Academy was transitioning to First State Military Academy, Scott responded to a fire alarm dispatch at the school. He waited in his squad for firefighters to arrive. As he was sitting in his car, the fire alarm ceased. It had reset itself.

"Now it's not supposed to do that. Someone has to go into the building and physically reset it," Scott said. The fire fighters arrived and accessed the Knox Box key, a lock box on the side of the door that the fire department can access when they need to enter a building. He entered the building with the firefighters, who of course asked Scott if he was the one that had reset the alarm. He told them he'd been waiting outside in his squad car, and furthermore, he didn't have the key to the Knox Box, so he couldn't have let himself into the building. The firefighters were confused; they couldn't understand how a system had been reset from inside of the building. Scott assured them that he'd arrived on the scene within two minutes of being dispatched. He'd been waiting in his squad car, and had not seen anyone enter or exit the building. There was no fire, and the alarm indicated that it had come in as an automatic fire alarm. "They were all blaming me, thinking that I'd reset it. I reminded them that I entered the building with them."

Scott no longer does shift work for the department, so he was unsure how often the local constabulary is called to the school to answer alarms any longer. He's been off shift work for four or five years now, about as long as First State has been in operation.

"It's one of those places that gives me goosebumps just to go to. And I always feel like I'm being watched when I'm in the [Drexel] building. The guys at the Fire Hall make fun of me, because I won't go into the buildings by myself. I wait for someone else to arrive and I go into Drexel *behind* them."

Scott admitted that his association with the school and its odd goings on started long before his tenure with local law enforcement. He was a young man when he first experienced the weirdness of St. Joseph's. The combined police and fire department had organized a Halloween fundraiser on the grounds of St. Joseph. He had taken leave from the military to return home to help his father run the event. His father was "big" on Halloween, and this event was his to run.

St. Joseph's Cemetery which is a hike into the woods. Surrounded by forest land, this sequestered location is the final resting place for many of the Brothers and Priests as well as lay people that were associated with the school.

He couldn't have picked a better location than St. Joseph's, as his son would attest.

The event was a Haunted Hay Ride and then a walking tour into the woods, with the final destination being St. Joseph's cemetery located in a wrought iron fence enclosed wooded knoll. After a short stroll in the cemetery, attendees would hike back out to the hay wagon and ride back to the parking lot.

At the pond where the hay wagon stopped, the event planners had set up four large generators where refreshments could be served and lights could be lit.

Scott and his friend, being in their early twenties, decided to play a bit of a light hearted prank on some unsuspecting soul. They were going to pretend to be "Jason" coming out of the water from the *Friday the 13th* movie series. As they lay on their stomachs by the pond, waiting to scare some unwitting soul into an early grave, the tables were uniquely turned against them. "As we're lying there by the water, all of a sudden all four generators shut down at once."

All four generators, Scott reiterated, ceased to work at the very same time, plunging the area into complete and utter darkness. The generators were of all different sizes and makes. One was a small, portable Honda unit. Another was a huge diesel generator on a truck. "It was just so strange that all four of them would turn off at the same time."

The event planners were busy restarting the generators. Scott said most of the attendees at the event were off on the haunted trail, and he didn't notice anyone meddling with the equipment.

It was then that Scott and his buddies noticed an eerie white light that seemed to be suspended over the pond. "It wasn't the moonlight or anything; it was a pitch-black night." Scott said that the mist seemed to be admitting its own light, and hanging suspended over the water. It was spherical in shape and condensed to the size of a beach ball.

Technically, this description is what researchers would define as an orb, a spherical ball of light that emits its own light instead of reflecting light from another source. True orbs can be seen with the naked eye versus appearing in a photograph, only to be noticed later. There is a lot of confusion regarding the phenomena, muddied further by the internet. However, what Scott is describing appears to be an actual orb, which is believed to be a ball of unexplained energy.

As Scott watched the white light, it began to slowly dissipate. He didn't wait to see it dematerialize completely. Sufficiently spooked, Scott and his buddy immediately left the woods and went back to the ticket booth, which was on the lot where they now park the buses. There he remained for the rest of the event. "I figured that something was telling us that they didn't want us there, and I got the message loud and clear."

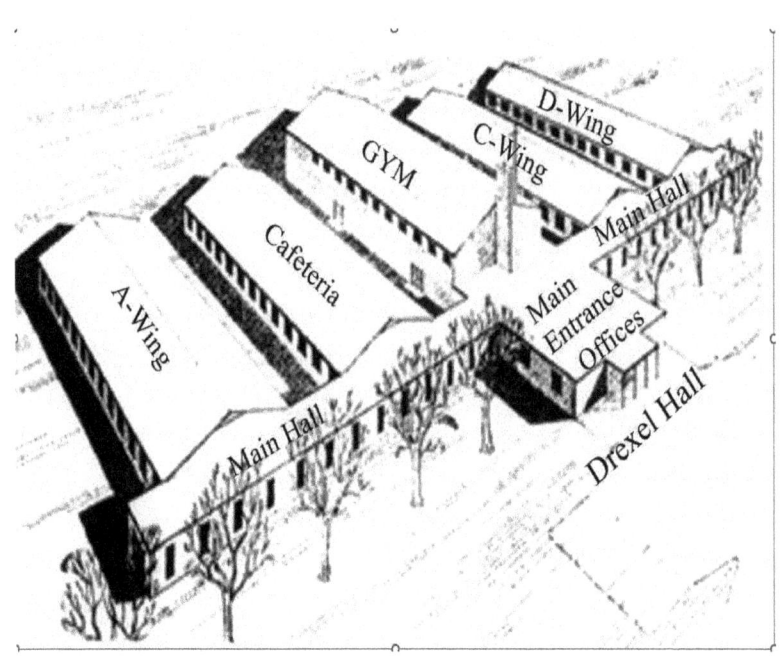

Chapter Four:
First State Military Academy

Janet Forrest,
Former School Office Director

After receiving an invitation to investigate, I began with a walking tour of the campus with Janet, now a former employee of First State. We started in Drexel Hall, which she admitted was a place, "where there is something about it that you feel." Note that everyone interviewed admitted that Drexel was a place where one never feels alone, that always creates a feeling like someone is watching them. It appears to be a universal observation of those employees, especially when they're in the building by themselves whether early in the morning or late in the evening.

The Main Office was a frequent location of strange occurrences, according to Janet. She noted that she was working one morning alone in the office and had the distinct feeling someone was watching her. She didn't see anyone, didn't hear anything, but the feeling that she was being observed by an unseen entity persisted.

She also recalled an afternoon when she and another secretary were working in the office when an odd breeze blew through the office at desk level. Janet noted that she could feel the wind brushing over her hands. The breeze blew past her and brushed over the hands of the other secretary as well. "It was significant; it felt like a breeze and it was moving."

Pens would also become airborne occasionally. They would be stationary on a desktop and then just fly to another location as if thrown. She noted that they weren't close to them when it happened either. "It wasn't as if we just hit them."

The ladies in the office also heard footsteps in the Main Entryway and the door to the office would open and close. They also heard banging in the basement directly under the office. This is the same basement where the man checking the sump pump had realized there was a figure behind him in the dark. The same basement where the Providence Creek Academy student had discovered the classroom that time forgot when down there for a tornado warning.

Computer screens will at times flicker. She said that just the day before, she and the other secretary were talking about the weird things that had happened at the school, but also the weird electrical disturbances Janet had experienced in her own home. It seemed to have stirred up some excitement in the office. Janet said that she had been trying to bring up a picture of a paranormal nature and the image was jumping back and forth between her two screens unaccountably.

Janet has had her share of paranormal experiences in the past, so she was very open to having the school investigated, as was, surprisingly, the Commandant of the School, Pat Gallucci, whose testimony follows Janet's. Prior to working at the school, Janet had operated a bakery in an old building in the area. The bakery's basement had been used as a stop on the Underground Railroad and renovations to the building had ramped up paranormal activity.

Being a bakery, Janet's employees, all young women, would work throughout the night. One morning, Janet recounts, she arrived at the bakery at 6:00 a.m. to find her female employees looking quite shaken. When she asked them what had happened, they recounted that they had witnessed a dark figure walk across three windows of the adjoining building, a restaurant then closed. This dark, menacing figure proceeded to come out of the building and stood on the walkway between the two buildings, staring into the bakery at the young women. According to Janet, an investigation of the bakery netted quite a plethora of evidence including a photograph of a young, African American girl.

Janet also recalled a brief visit of her deceased husband, a police officer who had passed of natural causes days before he retired from the force. He had died suddenly while in the master bathroom of their home. On the day of his funeral, Janet returned home and laid down in her bed. She hadn't slept in three days after having witnessed her husband's collapse and spent the subsequent time with him while he lay in the hospital on life support. She had been there when the hospital staff had disconnected him from the machines that kept his body alive.

As she lay on her bed, she saw her late husband come out of the bathroom in jeans and a t-shirt. He crossed over to his side of the bed and sat down and put his arm around Janet before disappearing.

After that, electrical disturbances began occurring in her home. Lights would turn on and off by themselves when no one was near the switch. She recalled that once, when her husband's fellow officers were in the dining room visiting with Janet, the light in the dining room came on for no foreseeable reason. The officers were stunned, but Janet, who was now immune to the strange activity, brushed it off.

One day she was attending a psychologist's appointment for grief counseling. The counselor's office played music on a ten-disc cd player. Suddenly the cd player stopped in the middle of the song it had been playing and switched cd's The new cd that started playing was Van Morrison, but the music didn't start playing at the beginning of the cd, but skipped to the song "Someone Like You," "which was a song that [her husband] used to play for me *all the time*." Not only was Janet surprised, but the psychologist was stunned as well, telling Janet that the machine had never done that before. At times the signs cannot be ignored.

We began the tour in the Commandant's office where Janet showed me the surveillance camera screens which at the time were black. The cameras themselves are motion activated, only turning on when they detect someone in the building. The Commandant had also told me that they had often turned on when no one else was in the building but himself. One would eventually capture the image of a dark entity, featureless, looking into Dr. Johnson's classroom while she prepared for class. Dr. Yasmith Johnson would eventually share that footage with me, in which there is an undeniable figure which appears to be staring in at her through the window of the door.

In the Commandant's Office I did have a reaction that I often get when in haunted buildings, that spine tingling hair on the back of your neck standing up reaction near the now dark surveillance screens. It was extreme enough for me to remark upon it, though I try not to give impressions until I've gathered evidence to support my personal experiences.

We continued down the Main Hall to the door of the basement. At the door my EMF detector registered a .4 and then a .6 MHz before returning to a 0.0. We looked for a source of electricity but found none in the stairwell to the basement. We also checked for an electrical box in the closet that was positioned next to the basement door and found nothing. The EMF spikes remained unexplained.

From there Janet showed me the notorious C-Wing where Dr. Yasmith Johnson had witnessed the figures of a priest and nun, and where Audrey had witnessed the dancers. There was a bathroom just as one turned onto C-Wing where the toilets often flush and the sink turns itself on and off. The plumbing fixtures are all on motion sensors. The room adjacent to the bathroom had been assigned to a coach at the school and a human resources employee in an office slightly further down the hall. Both have reported hearing the toilets and sinks randomly flushing or running.

Janet also shared that a teacher at the school named Skylar Hemsworth had seen the same figure of a man coming from the direction of D-Wing towards C-Wing. Not wishing to approach the figure, perhaps realizing that there was something off about the figure, Skylar just turned around and went the other way. Later, Skylar and Yasmith would discuss what they had seen with each other, and realized that they had witnessed the same man. Both described him as wearing tan pants, jacket and priest's collar, an older man with grey hair who would later be confirmed as Father Charles Brown.

During the tour we didn't visit D-Wing, as Janet didn't know of any odd occurrences ever being reported. Later I would find out that in room D-105 the lights would often turn themselves on. Once, when I was giving a presentation to First State students about the history and haunting of their institution, one of the students told me that he would be on the Quarter Deck looking down the main hallway and at the very end of the hall, where the turn off to D-Wing is situated, he would witness the lights flickering on and off, on and off. He didn't feel any desire to investigate, however. He stayed instead in the relative safety of the well-lit Quarter Deck.

We returned then to the basement door where I had just a few minutes earlier had the EMF spike. This time I got a .7 and then a .4 spike on the detector before it returned to a 0.0. That was twice now that I'd had the unexplained spikes. This time we descended into the basement. In the basement Janet told me they often heard banging noises, or the sounds of things being dragged or falling.

The basement at this time was used as a work out area with weights and weight benches proliferating the room. Exercise bikes and treadmills lined the back wall that led to the long tunnel-like crawl space. There was a good amount of electrical equipment and the notorious sump pump in the basement, any of which might account for the sounds. But Janet specified that it didn't sound like pipes banging, but like sounds of something being moved or kicked or something falling.

While in the basement looking at the utility crawl space, my EMF detector, which has an empod mechanism, sounded off for no apparent reason. It would do so again on my first investigation of the basement, in the same spot as it had that day.

Back upstairs we headed in the other direction to A-Wing, where Lauren had her classroom when the building had been PCA. Janet said that the activity seemed to be less regular on A-Wing with only an occasional eerie feeling being reported. All was quiet in the empty hall, and as Janet had very little knowledge of A-Wing, we departed it rather quickly and headed over the Chapel basement where more interesting phenomenon had been reported.

As we opened the doors to the basement and descended the slimy steps, we realized that the cement floor was partially flooded. Inside the basement were all the relics of St. Joseph's Industrial School. Old steel bed frames were intermingled with desks and chairs.

Moldering boxes of textbooks sat on the wet basement concrete floor, soaking up the moisture and spilling out their contents. Janet had never been in the basement, so she was as fascinated as I was. Here, truly, were the relics of the school that had operated for some 80 years before shutting its doors forever, leaving all its treasures to rot and decay. A sightless, statue of Mother Mary stood against a back wall with her arms spread to greet us. One of the books Janet found had a copyright of 1934.

I found an old prayer book on the floor, which I moved up to a desk to delay the decay. Old kneelers were in one corner. Hundreds of old bed springs riddled the ground and rusting desks were stacked everywhere. At the base of the stairs were memorial stones of marble, commemorating the deaths of individuals, both clergy and lay persons. Not being an expert on the Catholic religion, I can only assume they had once stood in the Chapel. It was a fascinating foray into the past.

Unfortunately, Janet found that she didn't have a key that would open the Chapel itself. She would have to get the key from the maintenance man who wasn't there that day. I would have to wait to assuage my desire to see into the building that had fascinated me since the moment I had seen it 15 years prior.

Once out of the very damp basement of the Chapel, Janet and I headed over to Morrell Hall, named still for St. Katherine Drexel's sister. This was the building where the Priest with the bible had been witnessed by the construction workers during Providence Creek Academy's renovations. In recent history, and since the renovations ceased, not a lot of activity has been reported in the building.

Morrell, like Drexel, had been extensively renovated and modernized. My EMF detector, as in the Chapel basement, remained at a stubborn 0.0. Large sunny classrooms with modern furniture were all that we saw. Even in the basement with closets full of combat boots and uniforms, we noticed nothing out of the ordinary. All of the electrical equipment had been updated and bled no EMF. It was a pleasant modern building, housed in the skin of a much older edifice.

Back in Drexel, we returned to Pat's office where I again got the chills, but didn't detect anything on the EMF detector. We took a walk around the old gymnasium. Having not spoken with the former Providence Creek Academy employees, Janet did not know the notorious activity that had been witnessed in that very gymnasium. That day it was quiet in the gym without even the noises that the team would experience during our investigations. From there we headed back down the main hallway, where I again felt something by the door to the basement, though the EMF detector now indicated a 0.0.

We did a walkthrough of St. Michaels where I noted getting a couple odd physical sensations on the camera I was using to record the event. These sensations I kept to myself. The school had undergone a complete renovation, and the classrooms were bright and airy with modern furniture. The EMF detector/rempod device registered a flat 0.0 throughout the building.

Having concluded the tour of the buildings, Janet and I discussed an evening to investigate. It would be soon, on a Saturday when the buildings were completely empty and we would have access to each and every area, this time including the Chapel.

Patrick Gallucci,
Former Commandant, First State Military Academy

Pat admitted that he felt something "off" about the buildings from the start of his tenure at the school. At the time he didn't feel it as much in Drexel Hall. From the beginning, most of the activity seemed centered around Morell Hall. Pat recalls the first time he entered the building. "I opened the door, and something just didn't feel right. That's when I saw a shadow [of a figure] move against the wall. I limited my time in there, especially when I was alone. I really didn't like being in there."

It wasn't until the contractors finished their renovations of Morrell Hall that the activity decreased in that building. During the renovations, the school often had difficulties keeping contractors on board.

Shortly after Pat's first encounter with the building, the water lines broke. They called in a local plumbing company to make the repairs. Afterwards, Pat was talking to the head plumber. Pat asked him about his time in the building and the plumber responded that he thought the building was "weird." Doors, in particular, that the plumbers would prop open would close on themselves. Still, the plumber, aside from not being able to account for the odd things that went on in the building, didn't attribute the happenings to anything paranormal, although Pat intuited to the man that there might be something beyond just closing doors plaguing the building.

A custodian in Morrell, one night following a school dance, was in his small work room in the building, when he distinctly heard what sounded like something being dragged across the cement floor in the basement. The sounds were so distinct that the custodian went to the stairwell and looked down into the basement. It was completely dark, but the sounds were distinctive. The custodian flipped on the lights, probably thinking that one of the students was still there. As soon as he flipped the switch on the lights, the dragging sounds ceased.

During renovations of Morrell, the contractors completely gutted the building, which undoubtedly disturbed the inhabitants greatly. Pat said he would often get asked by contractors who the priest was that walked around the building holding a bible.

Patrick assured them that there wasn't a priest on the payroll, to which they would respond, "we see the priest walking around with a bible." Apparently, he looked so life-like that the contractors never realized he was an apparition from a bygone time.

Once the building was fully renovated, Pat admits that the feelings he gets in the building have never been the same. He intimated that whatever spirit had inhabited Morrell, and whose peace had been disturbed, had given up and decamped.

Right off the front entryway (what the Marines refer to as the Quarter Deck) of Drexel was the Commandant's office. The lights in the main hallway were motion activated. When no motion was detected, the lights would time out and turn off. Pat often arrived very early in the morning to oversee the running of the school. He was often the very first person to arrive, often coming in as early as six or six-fifteen in the morning. He would pull up to the school to find that the lights were on in the front entryway. He'd worry that they'd been on all night, or that someone had entered the building. He'd park his car in the lot and walk to the front of the building, only to find that the lights were off. He remarked that there were no trees directly outside the building that would trigger the motion sensors. Indeed, what could be triggering the motion sensor lights was a mystery to him.

Eventually, Pat had the custodian remove the motion detection lights on the Quarter Deck and moved to light switches instead. Most of the electrical issues ceased. Pat mentioned the removal of the sensor lights several times during the interview. Apparently, they were a point of concern. Once removed, he was much more comfortable in the space. However, even with the motion sensor lights removed, he would often be standing at his desk in his office, again early in the morning, and notice that the motion lights outside the building would turn on. He would try to ignore them

Early on in his tenancy at the school, Pat was in his office, situated behind a small room that leads to the front Quarter Deck, which obviously obstructed any view to the entryway. One morning, Pat was in his office checking emails and getting ready for a busy school day when he heard footsteps walking across the Quarter Deck (front entryway). Then the lights clicked on. Pat was expecting his business manager, with whom he had an early-morning meeting scheduled. When Pat heard the footsteps on the carpet in the next room, he thought Asher the business manager had arrived. "Good morning, Asher," Pat called from his office. He didn't get a response.

"I paused a second, and then I walked out. Of course, his office was still locked and his lights were out. So, he's not there." The early morning experience left Pat very confused. He'd heard the light switch turned on, he'd heard the footsteps, and yet no one was there.

One Saturday afternoon, following an Open House, Pat was again working in his office. He was trying to get ahead a bit, before the rush came on Monday morning. From his office he heard someone walk down the hall. He thought it odd. After the event he had relocked all of the doors to the building and reset the security system. He knew he was the only one there. "I thought, how in the hell did someone get in the building?"

So, he left his office and proceeded out to the Quarter Deck and looked down the main hallway that runs the entire length of the building. Knowing he'd heard someone he proceeded to check the surveillance camera feed in his office. The cameras are motion sensor activated, and only record when someone is moving about in the area. "When they pick up motion they begin recording." Pat noted that the camera in C-wing had begun recording, although there was no one in view. Around ten seconds later the camera recorded Pat coming out of his office and looking for the interloper.

"I decided that day that I was going to grab my bag and go home. I knew there was no one else in the building. There were no cars in the parking lot." None of the other cameras had recorded any motion or anyone coming in the doors.

"You know, some mornings I would come in the doors, and it just felt like the building was…looking at me." It wasn't a presence that Pat found threatening or sinister. However, he noted that he felt a prescience in the building that detected him as well. Pat said that it was almost a comforting feeling.

The sounds of doors closing were another common occurrence Pat admitted he often heard, and one the team would record on our second investigation. "Sometimes in the morning I'll hear doors slamming. Always from the direction of C or D-Wing."

On the team's second investigation, in a clip taken from a video camera trained down C-Wing, first the rempod the team had stationed in the middle of the hall went absolutely berserk. When the rempod finally falls silent several minutes later, a door opening and closing is distinctly heard, the sound appearing to have come from behind the camera, which is the same general area where Pat explained hearing the door closing sound. There were no team members in the area at the time, and as the small team of four investigators were the only people on the entire campus that evening and all the doors were locked, remains unexplained.

Pat continued to report that when in his office he often heard things in the otherwise vacated building. Indeed, two weeks prior to our interview he noted that he had an experience. The stress of running a school often meant sleepless nights and early mornings. This particular morning, he was at the school before 6:00 a.m. The sun hadn't yet broken the horizon and the building was quiet and empty. He had gone into the bathroom adjacent to the Quarter Deck when he heard footsteps – out on the Quarter Deck itself. He left the lavatory to see who was about, and of course, saw no one.

Note the commonality of the interview with Audrey Erschen, the former principal of Providence Creek Academy. She reported also hearing the sounds of frequent footsteps in the front entryway when she knew she was alone in the building.

On the team's second investigation of the building, two of the team were conducting a session in the Chapel, and the other two, Penny and Marie, were in the gym. On the recording both Penny and Marie remark on the recorder that they distinctly heard footsteps out in the main entryway. They were so distinctive that the pair thought their teammates had returned from the Chapel and were now in the building. When Dave and I failed to materialize, the ladies continued to listen for more than six minutes to the sounds of footsteps moving around the Quarter Deck area leading into the gymnasium.

"Some of the things that happen are so small [mundane] that I don't even pay attention to them. My mind is on other things." Pat noted a couple of times during the winter months when he would arrive early and go into the bathroom. Of the two stalls in the bathroom, the one on the end by the window often seemed to have an occupant.

"A couple of times I could have sworn that there was someone in the stall." He'd hear sounds as if someone were moving about or a shuffling of feet. "Of course, being polite, I wasn't going to ask [if there was someone there]." Pat noted the Major often arrived early to use the gym for an early morning workout. But Pat, before departing, would look down under the stall for feet, and there were no feet to be seen. He'd simply leave.

Pat said that he felt it better not to acknowledge the activity, so as not to encourage it, as the Spanish teacher, Dr. Yasmith Johnson had done in the past. Still, he reported that he would often detect an energy, and he'd have a sense that something was about to happen. Usually, the occurrences were small, like footsteps in the hall or a shuffling in an otherwise empty bathroom stall.

Of Dr. Johnson's old classroom on C-Wing, Pat said he would sometimes observe the Spanish class. He'd be sitting in the room during class and he would hear the door handle jiggle. He'd asked a student close to him once if he had heard it as well, and the student replied, "Oh, Commandant Gallucci, it always does that." From what was told to me by the Providence Creek Academy people, those two rooms were always an area of activity, and apparently that didn't change when the school changed hands.

Pat did say that he would not go into the basement, at least not alone. "I look down in the basement, and I get an eerie feeling, and I just don't mess [around] with it."

Still, Pat admits that some of his fellow staff members never detected a thing in the basement or anywhere else in the building. The Major and the Assistant Principal often came early in the morning to work out in the basement, which is outfitted with exercise equipment. The two never experienced anything, and thought any such talk of spirits was absolute nonsense. Pat admitted that he felt that he and a few others on his staff were more sensitive to the presences, and couldn't discount them. Of the basement, in particular, Pat admitted that he "wouldn't want to be down there [alone] if the lights were to go out. "

The school administration contracted their IT work out with an outside company, and had decided to add six internet connections. The contractor assured Pat, so as not to get in the way of school functions, that they would come in at night to run the six additional lines to make the connections. There were three contractors in the building that night. Two of the contractors were in Pat's office where the main connections came in. Manny was in A-Wing, in the attic, in order to run the lines down through the wall. At one point Manny contacted Brian the contractor in the Commandant's office via a walkie asking why the third contractor, Shawn, was up in the attic with him, when he was supposed to be downstairs. Brian assured Manny that Shawn was standing right beside him in the Commandant's office. Manny was adamant that there was someone standing beside him in the attic as he was trying to run cables. The three elected to leave the building and come back during daylight hours to run the cables.

Pat recalled the time when a staff member, Skylar, reported to him about an experience. She had entered Drexel by the side entrance, from D-Wing to C-Wing. She had walked in the building and saw a figure strolling in the dark. Despite the fact that the building was dark, the exit signs illuminated the hall enough so that she could see the figure and discern that it was a man. The male figure walked from D-Wing down the Main Hall way and turned into C-Wing, and then stopped and looked at her.

Apparently, the figure Skylar saw was the fabled Father Brown, who Dr. Johnson would also see, and who was later identified via old pictures taken from the Chapel. Older Clayton residents who had attended services in the Chapel would help put a name to a face. Father Charles Brown had been custodian of the school for a number of years.

Skylar was so unnerved by the vision, that on this particular morning she turned around and left the building. She returned to her car where she remained until Pat arrived, and she could recall her story to him.

Skylar was also in her classroom on A-Wing when she distinctly saw a figure walk by her room through the window in her door.

Pat admitted that Skylar and Yasmith Johnson had identified the same person, the same Father Charles Brown. The same man was reported as wearing khaki pants, a dark sports jacket and a priest's collar by both women. Pat admitted that Skylar, "didn't like to talk about it."

The Commandant recalled that over the years of his tenure he's had many, many parents relay to him how "calm" [sic] and peaceful the campus feels. He admitted that they would tell him that the campus just felt, "different."

Of the activity, Pat said he saw it as a positive thing. It had been a boarding school for all those long years, and when the students were in the building, he felt that the presence liked it, that the grounds continued to be a school, an institution to change young minds for the better.

"And it does feel different. It's almost like the building itself has a life to it, the campus itself has a life to it. "

Dr. Yasmith Johnson,
Spanish Instructor

Yasmith came to the school in 2017 to teach Spanish. She was first assigned a classroom in St. Michael's, not a building normally known for its activity. She knew nothing of the school's supposed hauntings. She quickly started to suspect that there was something odd about the location. Her classroom, located on the second floor of St. Michael's, was particularly interesting as the desks seemed to have a will of their own.

It was after class one day when she carefully organized the student desks, arranging them all so that they faced the white board in nice neat rows. Job done, she headed toward the door to leave for the day when she happened to glance back at the room, only to find two of the desks had moved and were now facing toward each other, "like when two people are talking to each other." She never heard the desks move, certainly if they'd been pushed the sound would have been apparent. But she'd heard nothing. Returning to the desks, she again pointed them neatly toward the board. She checked again before locking the classroom. All was in order.

The next morning, she unlocked the classroom door and found the same two desks she'd rearranged twice the afternoon before, now facing one another again. This apparently happened repeatedly, and it was always the same two desks. However, she kept quiet about her observances.

At the end of the day, the students would leave and Yasmith would remain to grade assignments. At her desk, eyes down, she would often see, out of the periphery of her vision, someone standing at the door. She also reported the feeling of someone staring at her. "You know the feeling that somebody is there. I would [turn] my eyes and there would be nobody there." Yasmith reported that this happened every afternoon. "Every afternoon, yes, I see him."

Yasmith explains that she has been sensitive to such occurrences for most of her life. She noted that her mother had the same ability. It is not something that Yasmith likes to talk about, as she would really rather not have the gift.

"Honestly, I'm scared to see these things. I see what I see because I have to. I have no choice." Yasmith admitted she would really rather have someone to guide her with her abilities. Without guidance she prefers not to interact with the spirits she encounters, not wishing to take the risk. At the end of the term, the school administration offered Yasmith the position permanently. Yasmith at first tried to dodge the offer. She'd already seen and heard enough to make her wary of continued employment. The administration persisted and she finally agreed. They did move her classroom to Drexel Hall.

The classroom she was assigned was at the very end of C-Wing, the same wing where Chuck had witnessed the spectral cleaning man, and the area where he witnessed the boy running toward the school from outside – the boy that simply vanished. What she suspected about the school and the grounds would soon be confirmed for her irrefutably.

One very early morning Yasmith arrived at her classroom to start setting up for the day's classes. Like so many others that experience activity at the school, she often arrived very early and stayed late. This particular morning, she was in the classroom at 6:40 a.m. when she started to hear the sounds of the choir singing. She noted that the singing was simply beautiful and sounded like the singing of many voices. She had no doubt that it was the choir. "I thought Jennifer had to be crazy to ask the kids to come to school so early."

The choir room was located two doors from Yasmith's classroom. She assumed therefore that the choir was doing an early morning rehearsal. She left her classroom and walked to the choir room to ask the choir director why they were practicing so early in the morning. To her utter amazement she realized that the room was empty, though Yasmith could still hear the music. She decided to find Jennifer in her office instead. Jennifer's office was dark and locked. Not one to leave a mystery unsolved, Yasmith then said she went out to the parking lot to see if Jennifer's car was parked there. The teachers all parked in the staff parking lot, but Jennifer's car was not there. Still, Yasmith reasoned that Jennifer might have parked elsewhere. Later in the morning she did run into her colleague, and asked her if she'd been there early on. Jennifer responded that no, she hadn't.

"But I heard your kids singing this morning," a confused Yasmith told her.

Jennifer responded, "Yasmith, this school is haunted."

"What?" Yasmith asked.

"Yasmith, this school is haunted. I thought you knew that. Everyone here knows that this school is haunted. In my classroom the lights come on and go off. That's why I don't stay after 5:30 or 6:00 in the evening, especially in the winter."

Doing the interviews with former students of St. Joseph's, I asked them whether there was a choir at the school when they attended. I was told there wasn't. But it's inconclusive, throughout its many years of operation, whether or not St. Joseph's had once had a choir. Certainly, being a Catholic school there would have been singing during the services, and it's possible, and probably likely, that the nuns, priests, or brothers rehearsed music from time to time.

That was Yasmith's first encounter with C-Wing. She was soon to have another, even more disturbing experience. It was early in the morning on November 2nd, which Yasmith admitted was the Day of the Dead, although the dead were the furthest thing on her mind that morning, as she was rushing to her room to send out an email to parents for a field trip she was hoping to take her students on.

She was coming in the entrance closest to the Media Center. The Media Center was located in the small building next to Drexel Hall at the other end of the building from C-Wing. Keep in mind that all the wings are located off the long main hallway that runs the entire length of the building. Thus, from either end of the building it is possible to see to the other end of the building from the Main Hall. From her vantage point, as Yasmith was walking the hall toward C-Wing, she saw a man emerge from the door of the basement that she said used to be used by the priests. At first, she assumed the man was the maintenance man emerging from the basement, probably checking the sump pump.

But he wasn't dressed as a maintenance man. This gentleman wore a dark blue suit jacket over khaki pants. She wondered who he was and then a moment later a second question came to mind. Why was he walking so oddly?

The man was walking in the same direction as Yasmith ahead of her down the main hallway. Studying him, she realized he wasn't walking at all. His feet, she said, were not on the ground. Instead of walking, he appeared to be gliding down the hall, moving in the direction of C-Wing, where he made a left and disappeared from sight.

Yasmith admitted that she was shaking in fear. But she was on a mission that morning. There was an upcoming event for the students, and she had to get to her classroom to send out the urgent email message to the parents. There was no getting around it, Yasmith had to go to her classroom immediately, despite well-groomed, floating apparitions.

So, decision made, Yasmith turned left at C-Wing and saw the jacket-clad man she had seen before talking with a woman dressed in an old-fashioned nun's habit in the hallway of C-Wing. Neither were standing on the ground but appeared to be floating in midair. Now that she could see the man from the front, she saw that he was wearing a white collar around his neck like those worn by priests. She also noted there was something slightly odd about the pair, as if they were slightly darker than they should have been and semi-translucent. Yasmith's husky Spanish accent sometimes makes it a bit difficult to transcribe. She did say that he appeared human and yet not human, as if she could tell he was not a real, breathing man.

"As I told you before, I don't have any guidance. I don't know what to do when I see these things. So, I just said to myself, 'I don't see anything. I don't hear anything. I don't see anything. I don't need anything else.' I said that, and that's the way." She proceeded down the hall. She actually had to pass between the two figures to get to the classroom, but she did so by pretending not to see them. Visibly shaking, she unlocked her classroom door, went inside, closed the door, and started praying.

"At that moment, I didn't care about the email. I didn't care about the job. I just wanted to go home." She was terribly frightened, and yet she hesitated telling anyone about what she had seen not wanting anyone to think she was unfit for her duties.

Eventually, she spoke with a chemistry Instructor, Skylar Hemsworth. She told Skylar that she had seen a man. Without prompting the chemistry teacher described a dark jacketed, tan panted man with a priest's collar. Before Yasmith could say another thing. Skylar made it obvious she had seen the same figure.

During the team's first investigation at St. Joseph, while in the Chapel, Janet, still the school secretary at the time, found a poster board of old photographs. Instead of letting them molder in the abandoned building, she elected to take them back to Drexel and scan them. Many of the old pictures in this book were documented by Janet, a natural paranormal researcher.

When shown the photographs, Yasmith recognized one man. A grizzled, middle-aged priest with grey hair, wearing a priest's robe and wearing black framed glasses that seem to date him to the 50's or 60's. The man was photographed counting eggs in one shot, and standing in the center of a group shot with students and other faculty in another. This was the man that Yasmith and Skylar had seen. But identifying the man left us with one problem. While obviously a prominent figure at the school, we still did not know who he was.

But in this era of social media, I had an idea of how to unravel the mystery. I took a couple of the photos and put them out on my social media site.

Within a week, I had a name confirmed for my priestly gentleman, confirmed by two long-time residents of Clayton. Remember that the Chapel doubled as the Chapel for the school and for St. Polycarp's. Apparently, our prominent priest officiated at both masses and hence was known by the now elderly population, who identified him quickly as Father Charles Brown.

Now armed with a name, I wanted more information. However, more information was not forthcoming. I interviewed a former student of St. Joseph's, who remembered the Father and blithely described him as always pleasant. Remember, while the priests ran the establishment, it was mostly the brothers that had the most interaction with the students. So, my former student would only have come in contact with the kindly Father Brown at Mass.

Former attendees of St. Polycarp's in Clayton were not much more enlightening, never offering me more than a confirmed name. And thus, the trail ended abruptly. While disappointing, it is still an immense win. It's only rarely, as a researcher, that you get an actual identification of a figure witnessed and described in the same way by two people. Identified by photograph and named by life-long Clayton residents, finding Father Brown is a win. Why the elusive Father Brown still walks, or rather floats, down the halls of St. Joseph's is a question I may never be able to answer.

Inviting the Vampire In

It was in September that Yasmith committed what she described as a huge mistake. She had told her ghostly menagerie that when they were alone in the building, they could do anything that they wanted to do.

It was Friday afternoon, she reasoned, and the building would be empty all weekend, so she gave them, according to her, free rein to do whatever they wanted after hours. She felt that she had, by this suggestion, invited activity to escalate.

Former Commandant, Pat Gallucci, also seemed to echo that sentiment. He intimated, in our interview, that Yasmith had called down on herself much of the phenomena that she had then been forced to endure. During the interview I hadn't really understood what he meant. It wasn't until months later that I heard Yasmith admit as much during her own interview.

It might be argued that Yasmith appears to be somewhat of a magnet for activity, perhaps with heightened, innate ability to sense presences. Indeed, Pat speculated that she may have invited the disturbances by her recognition of the activity. There is a theory among paranormal researchers across the wide spectrum of phenomenon, that when one looks at paranormal activity, it will look back. Or, as it is said in vampiric circles, "never open the door and invite the vampire in."

A colleague, and fellow author of "Ghosts of Delaware," Mark Sarro recounted a home he had once owned in Pennsylvania. An older home, it seemed to have quite a bit of spectral phenomenality. Being an active member of a paranormal research group, Sarro decided to capitalize on the activity by placing the home on a haunted house walk that the group hosted. To spice things up a bit more, he placed surveillance cameras in various rooms around the residence, with the live feeds available to ticket holders. All the attention and scrutiny of the home backfired on Sarro, when he saw not only an uptick in activity, but began to experience far more sinister behaviors. At one point, he reported that he was in his bedroom, when an aggressive entity appeared in the door frame and openly seemed to stare Sarro down.

the cafeteria. She noted that the figures were smallish in stature, not the size of a small child, but too short to be an adult. Just like Father Brown, these figures appeared to be floating down the hall, not walking.

    Remember that St. Joseph's had been a school for middle-school aged children. What she seemed to be witnessing was a procession of students from the past moving from dormitories to the classrooms. She said the shadow figures moved in groups, and she estimated that there must have been 50 of these figures that she watched moving down the hall. She was adamant that the size of the figures was smaller than a high school student, but larger than a small child. She estimated the figures to be children of thirteen or fourteen. This would have been the age of the middle-school boys that attended St. Joseph's Industrial School. The number of students is also near correct. When St. Joseph's Industrial School was running, they would only house around seventy students at a time.

    Albert Einstein noted that time is not linear, as we, with corporeal bodies, perceive it. We, being physical beings, are born, grow up, mature, and grow old and thus perceive time as being something fixed. But it has been suggested that time may actually be layered and infinitesimal. Hence, the students of St. Joseph's Industrial School may be passing to class at the same time as First State Military Academy is conducting a ghost hunt in the old Chapel. With multitudinous timelines, what we perceive as spirits may simply be students moving to class on a different timeline.

    Another theory suggests that what happened in the past somehow gets recorded in the very fabric of a building or environment, often referred to as the Stone Tape Theory. When

In the upper frame is an image of Dr. Yasmith Johnson in her classroom. In the lower frame at the end of the hall is a dark, indistinguishable figure appearing to look in her classroom door window. Photo provided by Dr. Yasmith Johnson.

Ghostly Happenings Continue in C-107

In her early morning forays on C-Wing Yasmith noticed that the lights in Room 105 would often come on by themselves. Note the parallel to the motion-detector lights that Pat Gallucci noted coming on when no one was in the building. Lights that so unnerved him, he literally had them changed out with switches. Also recount the lights that blinked off in A-Wing that Leah noted, that not only affected the overhead lights but also the battery-operated CD player.

Often Yasmith would be working in her classroom, with the door to the hall open. She often noted seeing shadowy figures passing by the door. Once her dark shadowy figure appears to have been caught on a motion sensor activated surveillance camera. On the short clip you see Yasmith in her classroom. At the same time, at the end of the hallway, appearing to look in her room, is a completely black figure with no distinguishable characteristics. It's a rather chilling capture that certainly backed up her claims.

One morning during the Covid shut-down, she was at her desk which was located directly to the right of the door to the hallway. At the computer she was busily preparing for the online classes for the day, when she happened to glance up. Standing in the far-right corner of her room was a figure. She described the figure as looking like a monk, robed, and hooded. She couldn't see the face of the man as the figure appeared to be looking down, although she felt as if he was watching her. She also noticed that his hands were clasped, almost as if in prayer. And there he stood menacingly while she gaped in wild disbelief.

She knew she had to have reinforcements if she was to remain in the room. There was only one problem, the phone that rang the office was located on the back wall, but a few feet from the figure in the corner. She contemplated fleeing through the door which was far closer to her desk. She thought of opening the door and running to the next classroom for help. Why she didn't choose that route is rather a mystery, perhaps it was too close to the time that class was to start, or perhaps it was the fear of turning her back on the ghostly monk in the corner. She elected instead to go for the phone even though it would take her far too close to the specter for comfort. She reached the phone and immediately connected with Janet who was at the time the head secretary. "Janet, I need you to come to my office right now," Yasmith implored. "Come to my classroom and open the door. Open the door and do not close the door when you come in."

A bewildered Janet asked, "What happened Yasmith?"

"Nothing happened," she stammered. "Just come here to the classroom and Janet, leave the door open. Something is in here and it's right in the corner. "

As Yasmith put the receiver down the monk remained menacingly standing in the corner, and a strange wind swept past Yasmith. As she watched horrified, the wind appeared to tear the larger posters on the board. The posters were literally ripped off their staples and sailed down to the floor. She watched in terror as poster by poster was ripped from its staples and fluttered to the floor.

"I stapled those posters to the board. The staples came out like something was pulling them out. And I said, my God, what is this about?"

Janet, sensing something ominous was afoot, arrived with alacrity to find a terrified Yasmith. And now the smaller posters were suffering the same fate, becoming unstuck from the board, and rippling down to the floor.

Janet immediately asked, "Dr. Johnson, what is going on here?"

Yasmith asked her, "Do you see him? He is here."

"I don't see anyone. Who are you talking about?"

Though she could not see the dark figure that Yasmith was still seeing, a practical Janet started asking, "Who is here? Who are you? What do you want with Dr. Johnson?"

Yasmith asked her not to ask him anything, not really wanting to know.

As she looked at Janet, Yasmith noted that a small lock of Janet's hair was standing up as if someone was holding it airborne.

Not wanting to say anything to Janet to frighten her, Yasmith began to pray. "I didn't want to say anything to Janet, because then she would leave me all alone in there."

As they stood there, suddenly Janet looked over at Yasmith's computer. The cord had been pulled out of the back and the computer had shut down. "It should have been at full battery. But it was gone now, no battery, and the computer was off."

A terrified Yasmith had a class to teach in the classroom, although she really just wanted to leave. She quite frankly admitted that she was seriously considering never returning to the school.

Janet couldn't remain in the classroom with her, needing to return to the Main Office, so she talked to Ms. Kelly, the Human Resource Manager, to sit in the classroom with Yasmith.

In the afternoon, Pat Gallucci, the Commandant, came to check up on the frightened Spanish teacher. Yasmith felt defensive, probably not realizing that Pat had had his own experiences in the school.

"I know what you're going to say. That I am crazy. I am sorry, I don't want to talk about this because I don't want to sound like I'm crazy and I end up in an insane asylum."

Pat was sympathetic and implored her to explain what had happened. "Talk to me, Dr. Johnson. I know what you're going through because I have also had experiences in this building. So, talk to me. Tell me what happened."

She told Pat about the figure that she had seen in the corner, and the posters being ripped from the wall. Then she thanked him for the job, but explained that her husband was retired, and she really didn't need to continue to keep working.

"Dr. Johnson, follow me," Pat suggested. They left the classroom and went to an empty classroom on A- Wing. It was a larger classroom and it was on the quieter A-Wing. Pat promised it would be hers, if she just didn't walk out.

"I remained in C-107 for three more days [until her teaching materials could be moved to the new classroom] and let me tell you it was torture." The monkish figure would appear and disappear. "I would lift my eyes and it would be there." She tried her best to ignore it and concentrate instead on the students. She said it would most often appear to her when the students were not in the classroom. When the students were present and causing a ruckus was when she felt the most at ease. When they departed, however, the monk would reappear in his corner, keeping his spectral vigil.

For three straight days she saw this monk standing menacingly in the corner. She said he would stand there for an hour at a time, hands clasped, face peering downward yet watching her. At one point she broke a toe trying to run away from the classroom and the specter.

The toe was broken so badly that Yasmith had to have surgery. When she returned to school Janet called her into the front office, saying she had a gift for her. Janet gave Yasmith a Daily Missal from 1952, a copy of the history of St. Josephs, and the keys to A-108. A missal is essentially a Catholic prayer book. There were simply boxes of old religious books left behind when St. Joseph's closed their doors for the last time. Undoubtedly, Janet had found the missal on the premises and probably felt that the book might act as a token of protection for Yasmith.

Yasmith was startled and told Janet that the missal was not hers. But Janet insisted that she felt like the book belonged to Yasmith. Yasmith agreed and keeps it in her classroom, because it feels like a part of her, "like a finger on my hand." She now had a new home and a blessed talisman.

Yasmith admitted that it was much better in Room A-108, although she said she still feels like she's never alone. I spoke to the students at the school who are, of course, interested in knowing what the group uncovered in our investigations. During the talk, one of the young men said he'd been in "Dr. Johnson's room" just a few days beforehand. He'd been discussing something with Yasmith when the door to the classroom just inexplicably closed on its own.

A Free Mason Investigation

Yasmith recounted a small group that came in November from a Philadelphia Masonic Temple. The Masons had volunteered to help with some cleanup of the old Chapel. It was Janet's dream to save the Chapel, but without the one million dollars needed for restoration, the best she could do was clean it up. In payment for a day of labor, the Masons, one of whom was an amateur paranormal investigator, asked to do a ghost hunt in the old Chapel. They returned with a team of three, two men and a woman, and a local news crew.

As Yasmith had the most intimate experiences, they asked her to meet with the team, and to accompany them to the Chapel. Yasmith said she felt the group was a bit dubious of her claims. They asked her what she felt in the Chapel, and she informed them that she felt a presence by the old altar. They equipped Yasmith with a small REM monitor, a device that beeps when something breaks the electro-magnetic barrier around it. When Yasmith walked to the altar with the device in her hand, it started beeping crazily.

Yasmith then said she thought she saw movement up in the Choir Loft. Taking her lead, they went up to the Loft, and the REM device again started beeping madly. Having fulfilled her duties as ambassador to the spirits of the school, and feeling uneasy, Yasmith decided to let the team stay in the Chapel and she and Janet headed back to Drexel to wait in the office for their return. Yasmith noticed something odd going on in Drexel as they approached.

"Look, Janet, at the lights," she said. "Oh my God."

As they watched, the hall lights leading to C and D-Wing were turning on and off, on and off, on and off. She estimated that this pattern repeated itself six or seven times as the two women watched. Janet told Yasmith to go to the front office and just stay there. Yasmith admits at this point all she really wanted to do was go home. But she said she didn't want to depart immediately as it was raining heavily (which might attest to the activity that night, as thunderstorms are often believed to amplify paranormal activity.)

While sitting in the front office of Drexel with Janet, Yasmith said she was behind the front desk and looking through the windowed walls at the main hallway. For some reason unknown to Yasmith she began shaking unaccountably. The shaking was evident to Janet as well, who asked her what was wrong.

But Yasmith said she was incapable of speech.

"I don't know if you're familiar with shadow people?" What she saw were white figures with indistinguishable characteristics. They didn't have bodies, she noted, just thin vaporous figures that indicated bodies. As she watched in amazement, a small horde of these vaporous beings moved down the hall toward A-Wing and triggers are correct, such as the case with the storms that night, the images play out like a long-ago movie.

When the ghost hunting group finally returned from their vigil in the Chapel, Yasmith noted that the lone woman from the group appeared to be very pale and rather shaken. Yasmith knew immediately that something had happened to her.

Yasmith asked her, "Did someone touch you? She said yes, 'somebody touched my arm.'" In the news segment you see the group of three in the Chapel. The woman who was holding her arms folded behind her twitches visibly and then reported that she had been touched. After that occurrence, Janet recalled that the group stayed very close together. It's one thing to desire to witness something paranormal, and yet another to actually have it physically make contact.

Yasmith also said that, the night of the investigation, she saw what she described as green and purple balls, like big bubbles, moving from the main office across the front entryway towards what was then the Commandant's office. The door was shut at the time, and the balls of light appeared to move through the solid wooden door. She estimated that the balls were about the size of an orange, the smaller ones the size of a mandarin. Commonly referred to as orbs, these balls of energy are often seen in haunted locations. Please note, these are not to be confused with "orbs" that often show up on photos or videos. Those are typically dust particles or insects that reflect light as they move about an environment. For an "orb" to be considered an actual orb, they have to be able to be seen with the eyes and be self-illuminating, not reflecting a light source.

"Whatever it was," Yasmith admitted, "isn't hurting us physically." She did question as to why it was always her that saw these things, when she would really prefer not to, but the answer is probably her sensitivity, which could be considered a gift or a curse, depending on one's perspective.

She saw the shadowy figures of what we can assume to be shades of former students in November. In December she would see another child. The staff that year were putting together food baskets for the lesser fortunate students to take home. Yasmith had gone to the teacher's lounge, which is off the dining hall and nestled between the gymnasium to the right and A-Wing to the left. She had the intention of gathering some coffees to put in the baskets for the students to take home. She was handling the coffee packets when she saw a white bouncing ball in the room. The ball continued to bounce right through the door of the teacher's lounge which was shut at the time.

Intrigued, she went up to the door and looked through the glass. There, behind the ball, she saw a child of maybe 12 years of age (matching the age of the children that attended St. Joseph's.) The child was thin. She didn't specify whether they were male or female.

"You know, sometimes when I am scared, I can freeze or sometimes I have the energy to look beyond the situation." So Yasmith opened the door to look for the child and the ball that could bounce through solid glass.

Suddenly she heard a man ask her, "Dr. Johnson, are you O.K.?" The Commandant was there with the Dean of Students and the Assistant Commandant.

Knowing it was probably not the best time to recount her experience she just said, "I'm fine. I'm fine," brushing off the experience.

In January on an unusually balmy, sunny, winter afternoon, Yasmith was headed toward her car after work. As she approached her car, she heard someone call her by name.

"Yasmith, just like that." The students and the faculty always address her as Dr. Johnson, so she knew this was neither a cadet nor a faculty member. Then she heard the voice again, "Yasmith."

"I didn't turn around. I said, whoever you are, do not follow me. You do not have permission to follow me. I didn't invite you to follow me. Whoever you are, stay here." She got into her car quickly and left for home.

In Yasmith's words, "My last experience was last Thursday [April 2022]." She was in the faculty bathroom and had placed her classroom key on the windowsill in the stall for safe keeping. Suddenly she noticed that the keys were moving as if someone were picking them up. She was adamant that the keys didn't simply move around on the sill, but actually lifted, as if someone was picking them from the shelf. As the keys are quite heavy, according to Yasmith, there was no way to account for them levitating on their own.

"I thought, my gosh, my keys are moving…on their own. I'm not kidding you; I was in that bathroom for maybe one minute. I said, 'leave the keys alone, those are my keys.' I ended up washing my hands in the teacher's lounge. I was wondering what was happening? Am I getting used to this?"

Yasmith admits that the activity isn't as frightening anymore as when she first arrived. She's met a threshold where the events are commonplace.

Chapter Five:

Searching for Proof of a Haunting

Before beginning research for this book, I had a very limited understanding of the breadth and depth of the haunting of the school. I'd only had the walkthrough interview with Janet, who had told me of the odd happenings in the Front Office, the Commandant hearing footsteps in the hallway, the motion sensor activated surveillance cameras turning themselves on and the sighting of the Priest and nun on C-Wing.

The team that I direct works very differently than what you normally see on television. From years of experience, please know that there is almost always more going on in the background than the investigators will ever know. Therefore, my team relies heavily on recording devices, both audio and video. Knowing the magnitude of this investigation, I came heavily laden. We placed a camera on the Quarter Deck, one in the gymnasium, one shooting down C-Wing and another shooting down the main hallway towards C-Wing. Audio recorders were placed in the same places. One audio recorder was placed mistakenly in the cafeteria. It was supposed to be placed in A-Wing, but the investigator didn't know the difference.

The redundancy of a camera which records audio as well as video and an audio recorder might seem ridiculous; however, when an EVP occurs it will only occur on one device and not another. This is one anomaly that we use to help determine what is an actual EVP and what was a sound occurring in the environment, whether that be normal or paranormal. I also placed a video camera in the Choir Loft of the Chapel, and an audio recorder on the altar, which is still there, though the pews have long since been sold off. An audio recorder was placed in the Drexel basement as well to see if we could capture the sounds of items falling or being dragged. In Morrell, the building with the priest carrying a bible, we placed a stationary video camera and audio recorder and one rempod. Six video cameras and eight audio recorders all recording for several hours makes for an enormous amount of data to sift through. I knew going in that this would probably take the team several months to review, and so it did. But what we yielded from all those hours of hard work provided some of the best evidence ever collected in my entire career.

We also did significant research before going in. The team's researcher compiled a list of all of the deceased priests and brothers who had died and were buried on the grounds in the cemetery. I knew we were dealing with a priest, so we went in armed with possible names.

We got our first EVP during setup. The team was scattered, setting up equipment not only in Drexel, but Morrell, St. Michael's, and the Chapel. With a multi-building set up, obviously the team is dispersed rather sparingly. Hence, I was alone in Drexel setting up a table and chairs from which to install the 4-camera surveillance system. In the EVP, one of the most extraordinary of my career, one clearly hears a male tenor singing.

No one was on C-Wing at the time, and certainly no one was around that had the propensity of breaking into song at a moment's notice. The noises from the front entryway are me setting up a table and chairs in the Main Entryway of the building. Suddenly the voice recorder in C-Wing captures what sounds distinctly like a male with a pleasing tenor voice belting out a series of notes, completely unbeknownst to me. In the way of EVP's, I was completely unaware that anything of that magnitude had just occurred. What I especially love about this EVP is that it backs up the activity Yasmith reported during her interview. Clearly, music is a common theme amongst the spirits of St. Joe's. Whenever we are lucky enough to capture evidence that correlates closely to an eyewitness report, we're obviously ecstatic. It makes both the anecdote and the evidence that much stronger, simultaneously.

We caught another EVP again during setup. My young female investigator was placing an audio recorder in the cafeteria when a male voice is clearly heard whispering the word, "ditto." She was the only one in the room at the time. A male was accompanying her, but he never entered the cafeteria but stood outside in the hall waiting for her to return. I can only imagine whoever was watching all of the equipment peppering the building felt the need to remark on the redundancy.

Setup complete, the squad broke up into teams of two or three. The plan was to disperse to different buildings and areas for an hour and then switch locations. In this way we could cover more ground and also not contaminate any evidence with too many investigators in one area, a constant source of concern.

I've worked with people that are overzealous at times. They feel the need to be constantly moving, constantly speaking. If they're not thinking, they'll start whispering, and it gets picked up and mistaken for an EVP. Or they speak too loudly and drown out the sounds in the building.

We did an investigation one winter in an old building under major renovation. The night was frigid cold, and all we had was a propane heater with a very loud fan. It was either freeze all night or run the heater to try to stay warm. We chose the latter, but all we heard throughout the night was the heating system running. It was a waste of an evening, and I contracted a sinus infection afterwards anyway.

Audio contamination is always a concern. One of my best investigators is also an avid hunter, so he speaks softly and minimally. He knows how to stand in a space and quietly observe. Whether you're up a tree stand in the early hours of the morning, or in an empty building trying to entice something to interact, the concept is the same.

It's a myth, especially promoted on television shows, that a presence in the area will desire to interact with investigators. I've found that more often than not they want nothing to do with us. I caught an EVP once in a closet that said, "Yes, I see him." The closet had doors to the hall and the bedroom. It appeared the female entity was actually in the closet peering into a bedroom, gazing upon the one male investigator we had with us that evening. Apparently, she had no intention of interacting with him.

We caught another EVP in the bedroom of a townhome that said, "They can't see us." This was followed by another female voice that confirmed the observation saying, "No," as in "no they can't see us." The two investigators were on the other side of the room from where the audio recorder was stationed. Again, it appeared that the entities were keeping their distance. Over the years I've also caught plenty of EVP's that say things very much along the lines of the Hartly House female who told us quite frankly, "You can go. You can go *now*."

Conversely, I had another investigator that was a chatterbox. She just couldn't *not* talk, mostly about topics that had nothing to do with the investigation. Oddly, that often worked in our favor, because I think the entities got jealous that she was taking up all the attention. We were sitting in the bedroom of a haunted hotel one evening. Once again, my fellow investigator grew quickly bored with observing and trying to interact. She had launched into another conversation when suddenly the rempod we had sitting on the table just blared one really loud blast. The noise was so jarring it catapulted me from my chair. It was as if to say, "Stop it. You're supposed to be paying attention to me."

So, we had four buildings on this investigation, plenty of space to fill out. I teamed up with Dave on this investigation. Our first destination was C-Wing, as it was obviously the most notorious. We took our list of deceased priests and brothers and attempted to make some contact. We read the names slowly with plenty of time in between to see if we got a response. We read through the list two or three times but got no response from what we observed. Nothing was caught on the audio recorder or video either, though we wouldn't know that until evidence review.

From there, we entered Yasmith's classroom, the space where all the posters were yanked off the walls. We sat in the dark room and tried to make contact again, again with no success.

From there we headed to the gymnasium and Quarter Deck area. I didn't know at the time that the gymnasium was a spot of high activity. I wouldn't gain insight into the strange happenings in that location until after the investigation, when I spoke with the PCA people.

But the old gymnasium had a nostalgic feel that drew me in. It had been original to St. Joseph's and was still in use. Dave and I moved about the gymnasium for a few minutes, taking readings and trying to entice something to visit with us. Finally, we moved to the back of the gym where there is a stage. From the stage we could see the entire gymnasium and out into the Quarter Deck, so it was an excellent vantage point. We sat on the stage and again tried to engage something to make contact. This is when the evening got a lot more interesting. We both started hearing creaking sounds and also what sounded like footsteps on the floor of the gym at the far end of the gymnasium.

In the video of the event one hears an initial cracking sound, followed by two creaking noises like a footstep. I then ask, "Is that you walking?" The noises seemed to start at the back of the room but then move to one side of the gymnasium. A few moments later it sounded like it had moved again to the back of the gym. I ask it if it would like to walk towards us, inviting it to come closer. It didn't, however, but seemed to wander around to one side and then back to the entrance before moving to the other side, as if something were pacing around us, but keeping its distance.

"It's a lovely old gym," I said, after which there is an immediate cracking sound.

"Did you have lots of games here?" I asked, after which we hear a small noise, seemingly in response to my question.

I followed up my question with another question. "Did you teach here?" Again, we got a cracking sound.

Thinking I was on to something, I asked, "Were you a priest?" To this question the room went silent. At the time I didn't know that the priests didn't teach the boys, but that the teaching was left solely to the brothers. If the noises responded affirmatively to the question of whether they taught, but not to whether they were a priest, it all makes much more sense to me now.

"Why have you stopped moving around?" I asked after a couple of minutes of silence. "We would love to make your acquaintance." This was followed immediately by a louder, cracking noise.

"We came here just to see you," I cajoled. "This is a lovely old gym; this is a lovely old school." We heard a creaking sound. It was then that I decided to announce to the room that I had been a teacher too.

"I used to work with youth. I was a high school teacher. I used to love molding those young minds." This was followed quickly by a sound to the side of the gymnasium that appeared to be much closer than the other noises had been. And then another small sound.

After that the sounds again appeared to stop. I again asked if it had stopped moving around. I then reminded it of the audio recorder sitting on the stage, and asked it to leave a message that we could then pass onto the folks at First State Military Academy.

More silence followed, and then I said to Dave, "The sounds have stopped now," followed immediately by another sound. Then more silence. "Can you show yourself?" I implored, after which we got two cracking noises as if it was a footstep with the heel hitting first followed by the toes.

At this point I began questioning whether it was just the sound of old wood cracking. However, if that were the case it would be making the sounds sporadically and often. When the sounds stopped, there was no other sound in the gym. And when the sounds were present, they appeared to be interactive to my questions and moving about the room.

"We won't bite," I told the sounds, "We just came to visit." This was followed by two footstep sounds, this time all the way to the back of the gym as if departing.

After that, though Dave and I spent more time in the gym, we got no further noises or seeming interaction. Another team that evening had a similar experience of hearing footsteps in the gymnasium, but they hadn't thought to bring an audio recorder with them, and so we have no recordings of their experience. The footsteps, again, were extremely similar to what had been reported to us by Janet and Pat Gallucci. They both reported often having heard footsteps on the Quarter Deck when no one else was in the building. The entrance to the gym lies right off the Quarter Deck.

Penny and Kayla replaced us in Drexel when the teams rotated. In the basement of Drexel, Penny seemed to have ruffled some feathers. In one corner of the basement is a section of metal fencing closed off and locked so that the school can store items and not have them stolen. The two were sitting on the weight benches near the metal cage.

Penny was making it a point to suggest that perhaps the ghostly priest was seen with the nun in the hall on C-Wing because the two of them had been intimately involved.

Unbeknownst to me, having not grown up in the Catholic church, such liaisons are not uncommon among the clergy. It would not have crossed my mind to ever have made such an accusation. But Penny did and, immediately after making the suggestion both she and Kayla heard the metal cage rattle.

Kayla who was leaning back on the cage also reported feeling it vibrate. Sadly, the audio recorder in the basement did not pick up the sound. When Dave and I were in the Drexel basement, my Mel Meter again sounded an alarm on the EM pod device in the exact spot that it had when I had done the walk through by the exercise bikes near the entrance to the crawl space tunnel.

Our time in Drexel up, Dave and I headed over to the Chapel, taking Janet with us. In the Chapel itself we had only one small personal experience, though evidence review would offer us a plethora of other evidence. We were in the Chapel, when Janet reported the feeling that there was a cobweb over her face. The ceilings are extremely high in the Chapel, and it's very doubtful she would have run into a cobweb, but it is a feeling often reported in haunted locations.

Another team investigating the Chapel that evening would tell me of a remarkable experience sadly uncaptured. As it had been an old Catholic Chapel, Penny, raised Catholic, placed her rosary on the altar stone, which is a piece of marble inlaid into the altar. She had a small box that she placed on the stone and then she placed the rosary around the box. The two then went up to the Choir Loft. When they came back downstairs. For some unknown reason the two stayed in the Chapel only a few minutes and then decided to leave the building and walk around outside. When they returned to the Chapel, Penny walked back up to the altar only to find that her rosary had moved and was no longer in the position she had left it in. The rosary that had been placed around the box was now lying across the box. The camera that was in the Choir Loft shooting down on the building was obstructed by a hanging chandelier in the center of the room and did not record the movement. An audio recorder on the altar itself did not detect any sound of the rosary moving. Unfortunately, the event remains undocumented and thus unprovable, though Penny was adamant that the rosary was in a different position when they returned. We instigated a new rule in the group after that disappointment. Now if we lay a trigger object down, we take a photo of it, and then if it has moved another photo or two to confirm that the object moved.

There was also a voice, distinctly female, captured in the Choir Loft that pointedly told Penny and Kayla that they were somewhere they shouldn't be. As the two approached the altar, the female can be heard clearly saying, "You don't belong in here."

The camera that I had in the Choir Loft was on a tripod five feet above the ground shooting down on the Chapel. I had it on a battery pack and it recorded for hours that night. Upon reviewing the footage, I noticed immediately that there were all sorts of activity in the building that night. Indeed, it seemed excessively fascinated by the camera.

Several times on the feed, we got what sounded like something rubbing or scratching at the camera near the microphone. Then I started to notice strange camera movement as well. Sometimes it would move horizontally, slightly back and forth. Other times it would seem to move vertically in one direction and then move back vertically the other way, truly remarkable evidence. If the tripod had shifted for some reason the camera might tilt down vertically, but there's no accounting for it moving up vertically in the opposite direction.

One time it actually appeared as if the camera zoomed slightly, which of course has to be done manually. It did appear as if the camera was being manipulated at the device itself. If it had been an animal, such as a raccoon for instance, it most likely would have come in contact at the base of the tripod, bumping it. And we would have heard the movement of an animal on the audio feed approaching and then departing. There were no such animal noises. The camera movements and the rubbing sounds happened both when investigators were in the building, and when the building was empty.

Being short on cameras, we had only one extra audio recorder for the Chapel basement. It caught only one thing that evening, but it was a remarkable catch. Being short on personnel, we had invited a couple of investigators from the Wilmington area to join us that evening. They had been accompanied to the Chapel by Janet. You can hear them upstairs moving about and then there is a distinct sound of what sounds like a little girl giggling. Knowing that Janet, a female, was in the building at the time, I decided to take it along on the reveal and ask her if that was her giggling. She was floored when she heard it and was quite adamant that it wasn't her, and that wasn't the way she sounded when she laughed. It does sound distinctly like a child's voice and was reminiscent of what Officer Harvey had told me in his interview about the ghostly giggling that kept them running around the Chapel searching for a lost child that wouldn't be found, although I wouldn't know that until several months later.

I was the one that reviewed the Chapel video footage. Several times, I would detect what seemed like movement out of the corner of my eye. This phenomenon is reported to me all the time by witnesses, but was not something that I had ever actually experienced myself. But as I was watching the feeds, out of the corner of my eye I would sense movement. I would stop excitedly and then review and rereview the footage to try to see what appeared to be moving. I'd sit and stare for long minutes in the area where I thought I'd detected movement and see nothing further, chalking it up to my imagination.

When we did the reveal with the First State personnel, Commandant Pat Gallucci and Janet, they tethered my laptop to a large flat screen T.V. There on the large screen, as we watched the footage from the Chapel, Pat suddenly remarked, "I saw something moving." I was shocked, as I hadn't told them of my experiences when reviewing the feeds. We stopped and backed up the recording, and on the excellent quality, large screen T.V. I could finally witness what had been eluding me on the smaller screen, something mainly transparent but still with form, moving about the area near the altar. All of us could see it and trace the movement. I was vindicated.

As Pat had told me, Morrell Hall seemed to have quieted down since renovations were completed. While we had a camera and audio recorder in Morrell Hall that evening, and teams moving in and out of it, there was only one report of the Rempod going off. Nothing else was caught. As Pat had said, after the renovations were done, Morrell is mainly quiet now.

Late in the night, Dave and I, who had done a tour of Drexel, Morrell and twice in the Chapel, were going out for a final placement in the Chapel when Janet asked me whether we'd like to take a stab at St. Michael's instead. I'd had a student football player send me a photo from the basement of St. Michael's with a supposed figure in the background.

Two football players in the basement of St. Michaels with what appears to be an ethereal form behind Player 16.

As we had surveyed every other building, we agreed and Dave and I headed off to St. Michaels. We did a quick tour of the building and then settled ourselves in the basement as that is where the activity had been reported to me as occurring the most frequently.

We had no experiences in the basement, and nothing was recorded, though we did our due diligence.

What struck me, however, were the pipes. There was water constantly running through the pipes. Why in an empty building would there constantly be water running through the plumbing? Completely baffled, I made a point of asking Janet when we returned to our headquarters in Drexel. The answer provided the first revelatory insight as to why the school might have so much paranormal activity. Janet explained that St. Michaels and Drexel were both built on an underground river. If you know anything about water, it is very often present in places with reported paranormal activity. It appears that water, or perhaps the minerals in the water, somehow record images from the past and replay them or that water somehow fuels activity. It seems that that underground source of constantly flowing water keeps the school flowing back and forth perpetually in time.

After our stay in the St. Michael's basement, it was time for Dave and I to depart. We came up the stairs, equipment in hand, and I stopped in my tracks. I heard voices, quiet but distinct. I thought at the time, the sound being so faint, that it was children outside playing, despite the hour being quite late. Just to make sure I went to the front door of the building and looked outside. There were no children or anyone out and about. But I had definitely heard voices. Unfortunately, my audio recorder was either not recording at that time, or it didn't catch the voices that I had heard. Sadly, it was just another personal experience on an eventful evening at First State Military Academy.

During our reveal to First State personnel, they were pleased with our results. Pleased enough, it turned out, to have us back to investigate the school the following summer. By that time Janet had left her employment at First State, electing to stay home with her two adopted children. The Commandant, Pat Gallucci, let us in and gave us the keys to the kingdom and the rest of the night was ours. He had intended to stay the night and investigate with the team, but something had come up, and he couldn't remain. We were a lean team of four, and we had the entire campus to ourselves. It was a paranormal researcher's dream come true.

Chapter Six:
Return to First State

Having delivered so little on the first investigation, we decided to forego Morrell and the time it would take to investigate and review. We skipped St. Michael's as well, as it had produced very little except the voices that I had heard but not captured. We were a small team that evening, having not invited another group in to assist. We were a force of only four, including Dave and Penny for a return trip. This time Marie accompanied us as well. Marie is one of my favorite investigators as she is very grounded in science and strong in common sense. She isn't a thrill seeker and does her homework, two attributes I value highly.

It was Marie who actually told me that she'd been researching weather patterns that night and that there were supposed to be solar flares. Anything that might fuel further paranormal activity is of interest of course, and I was excited when she told me of the events.

From my brief research on solar flares, it appears they occur when electrically charged gasses twist and stretch and then, in a brief explosive eruption, are released from the sun's surface, sending a burst of electro-magnetic radiation into space.

According to a *Nasa Science* article, an extremely strong ejection can interrupt radio communications. They can also interfere with utility power grids.

At their very strongest, they can cause electrical shortages and power outages. Now solar flares do not make it all the way to the Earth's surface but are caught in the Earth's ionosphere; however, the flares, if strong enough, can affect the Earth's magnetosphere (Tingley, 2022).

The classification of solar flare strengths begins with A and B class flares being the weakest. M class flares are somewhere in the middle, with each class being 10 times stronger than the class below them. Class X are the strongest and most disruptive on Earth. While the strongest emissions, they occur only around 10 times a year. Researching further, I noticed that on July 17, 2022 there was a warning from Kirkland Media of X Class sun flares, which can "create long-lasting radiation storms (Powerful Solar Flare, 2024)." Space.com posted an article on July 22, 2022 that confirmed the solar storm would continue on Friday night and continue into the early morning of July 23, 2022, the date of our investigation (Dobrijevic, 2022).

It was indisputable that the team was registering high electro-magnetic disturbances that evening that had not been evident on the first investigation. It's also possible that this energy fueled the paranormal activity on the second investigation. While the first investigation had been exciting, the second would prove a powerhouse.

This time during setup three of my investigators were on the Quarter Deck, setting up equipment, chairs and tables. I had gone into the gymnasium where there was better lighting to fight with a GoPro camera that was giving me a difficult time.

There's never an investigation where one piece of equipment or another doesn't try my patience. While I was in the gym, grumbling over the GoPro, all three of the investigators clearly heard a male voice emanating from the main hallway leading to A-Wing, and it appeared to be laughing at them. Perhaps it remembered our first bumbling attempts at capturing evidence the year before, perhaps it was just being friendly.

All three of them heard the laughing voice, but I, being in the gym, did not. It was an auspicious beginning. Sadly, it being set up, there were no recording devices yet up and recording, so the laughing specter, while heard by three people, was not recorded.

The Quarter Deck that evening took on a life of its own. There were constant EMF spikes occurring that evening. We had the lights off on the Quarter Deck and there was nothing else giving off electromagnetic energy that evening, yet EMF spikes were almost constant. The team did their due diligence and took readings of the lights and wall mounted heating units. None were operating, and were giving off no readings.

I had taken my Mel Meter out and set it on the table we had set up. Seven minutes and fifty-two seconds after setting up the rempod on the table sounds, and my Mel Meter which was also on the table, spiked up to a 19.7 and froze there. I've never experienced a spike like it before or since, even off man-made devices like a microwave oven.

I had to take the meter outside, remove and replace the battery, and turn it back on before it would actually function again. Honestly, I was worried at the time that the spike might have fried the meter's circuits.

Penny was also registering EMF spikes and announcing them to the camera. .5, .4, .3 and then back down to a 0.0. We ran an experiment to see if the EMF detector would respond to voice commands, and it did several times. It's a technique where you ask a question and ask that an entity respond by making the meter register EMF. On this night the meters were responding to voiced questions.

At 11 minutes and 38 seconds on File One of the Quarter Deck footage I notated that it sounds clearly like a footstep on the deck. I must have heard with my own ears at the time because I said clearly, "ah, there you are."

Remember, Pat said that footsteps on the Quarter Deck occurred quite frequently, which he heard from his office. It seems we were experiencing much the same.

The video camera recorded in 20-minute segments before starting a new file. In the second file noted in my log, we were trying to figure out knocking sounds we were hearing. And again, I noted that the EMF meter sitting on the table was registering EMF spikes of .3, .2, .1 and back to 0.0.

Set up complete and already experiencing odd manifestations, I decided to take a lone trek to A-Wing. Marie and Penny headed toward C-Wing, where they also reported a lot of remarkable EMF spikes as well. On the recorder, Penny is recorded in the long hall reporting a 2.1 spike.

Dave wandered about between the gym and the basement. Dave is a new investigator and has those tendencies of wanting to be everywhere at once.

I was pleasantly surprised at A-Wing that evening. We hadn't placed any equipment on A-Wing on our first investigation, as the audio recorder had been mistakenly placed in the cafeteria instead. We had sent investigators to A-Wing that night with hand-held devices, but the team reported no EMF spikes, no experiences, no evidence at all. This night, whether it be the solar flares or not, A-Wing just had a completely different feel; it just seemed to be alive that evening. We'd already heard the disembodied voice coming from the Main Hall that led to A-Wing.

Unbeknownst to us at the time, on the voice recorder placed on A-Wing, we had captured an EVP already. It was a distinctly male voice in a completely deserted wing. In the EVP a male voice is heard quite distinctly saying, "Ball get." The voice is clear, the EVP clearly a Class A, perhaps a residual sound of a long-past basketball coach? We research the paranormal for glimpses and answers from the past, and sometimes all you get is a completely innocuous, inane EVP saying "ball get."

With the random EMF spikes on the Quarter Deck already noted, and the disembodied male voice from the main hall running towards A-Wing, I decided to take a solo sojourn down the Main Hall toward A- Wing. While in the Main Hallway I was registering EMF spikes of a .5, and then a 0.0. I was concerned that the EMF might be the wall air conditioning unit that was on and blasting cold air. Still, it was sporadic enough. In other words, I didn't just get a steady reading as you ought to if you're reading an electronic unit, which piqued my interest.

I continued on my way and turned in on the dark, quiet, deserted A-Wing. In the middle of the hall, I registered on the voice recorder in the hall a quick .5 and then a 0. One minute later I noted a .1 and then back to 0. I entered a classroom that was standing open and standing near the doorway of the empty, dark room, exactly one minute after that the meter registered a .5 in the hall, the meter seemed to take on a life of its own. I voiced the readings to the recorder as I read them and I reported a 1.8, 1.5, 1.3, 1.5, .8, .9, 2.0, 1.4, 1.5.

At this point I decided to try an experiment. I've only ever seen this work on a television show once. But I decided to see if the meter would respond to my request. I asked it out loud, "Can you give me a reading of exactly 2.0 on my meter?"

For one brief moment the meter registered a 2.0 exactly as I had asked. And then it continued its merry dance of a 1.4, 1.5, .8....

Sometimes it seems that entities like to keep their distance. Therefore, I decided to set the meter down on the ground and backed away a couple of feet to give it its room. The meter continued to register spikes in an empty room with no lights or electronic devices operating .8, .7, .6, .7, .6, .7, .7, .6, then for a while it got stuck at .6. I never thought about it until now, but the fact that it was repeating .6 and .7 over and over might have been its way of demonstrating to me that it could in fact control the meter readings. At the time I didn't get the joke; I was still stuck on the fact that it had given me an exact 2.0 right after I had requested it do so. That just doesn't happen. As Renee Zellweger said in *Jerry Maguire* "It had me at 2.0."

Tiring of the .7's and .6 spikes, it began to do a far more random pattern again, registering .9, 1.0, .8, .5, before returning to a 0.0 and remaining there. A minute later on in the recording, I reported having the chills, which appears to be my body's response when paranormal entities are near. This was an extremely hot evening, and the AC unit wasn't running in the classroom at the time (I recorded all of these facts in my log book), so there shouldn't have been any reason why I should feel chills and yet I was.

My interest thoroughly aroused, I returned to the Quarter Deck to try to convince the rest of the team to follow me back to A-Wing. Marie has that clinical, more scientifically based approach to research that I so value, and I really wanted to get her opinion of the EMF spikes.

When I returned to the Quarter Deck the other three were there and the odd EMF spikes were continuing to spark their interest. While we stood there the meter on the table registered a 2.5 and a .8. Having been successful on A-Wing, I again asked it to register exactly a 2.0. Quickly afterward the meter again registered an exact 2.0. Then it shot up to an 8.8, 8.9, 8.6, 3.1, 2.6. You may be wondering why we were so excited by the spikes. If it had been EMF from an electrical source such as unshielded wiring, the EMF that registered would have remained steady, and this was all over the place. Further, when we get anomalous spikes during investigations, it's usually very minor such as a .1 or .2, only rarely do we catch something as high as a 1.0. These spikes were off the charts and we knew it. Not only that but all the lights were off.

We also noted that when we spoke about the fact that we were heading toward fall, the EMF meter would seemingly spike. Perhaps the entity was looking forward to fall and the return of the students to the school.

However wild the ride was on the Quarter Deck; I did want to get the team down to A-Wing. As we headed down the Main Hall, I showed Marie where I was getting spikes. There was a wall AC unit near the location. Marie agreed they were curious, but the proximity to the unit made the EMF spikes suspect. And when we parked the EMF detector directly below the unit, we realized that it gave off a steady 2.4. We decided at that point to disregard any readings near the unit as EMF discharge. Mystery solved, the team entered A-Wing and Dave actually recorded a couple of spikes on his recorder at two hours into the investigation of a 1.3 and a 1.7. Approximately four minutes later he noted a spike of a 4.4 on the EMF meter before it returned to 0.0. Two minutes afterwards, I verbally reported feeling chills again. While we had debunked the AC unit, these we could not account for, as all the lights and electrical equipment in A-Wing was turned off.

Late in the night on A-Wing, with no one but the team on the premises and absolutely no one in A-Wing, the voice recorder caught one of our most idyllic EVPs of all time. The hallway is empty and dark, as is the main hallway. It is so quiet in fact that all I could hear on the audio recorder was the ticking of a wall clock. I'd spent hours listening to empty audio in which all I could hear was tick…tick…tick…

Then suddenly, out of nowhere, came the sounds of shuffling feet, and a male voice whistling and mumbling to himself. It's as if a custodian came down the hallway shambling and whistling to himself, and then turned in somewhere. After this brief interlude, all I could hear was the ticking of the wall clock. The sounds of a shambling custodian had seemingly come out of nowhere, and disappeared too nowhere.

What makes this so astounding is that the team had the entire campus to ourselves that night. We saw no other human being after Pat departed. Even if it had been a lone custodian that had entered the building unbeknownst to us, he would have had to come out of the room he had entered and left the building at some point. And yet, all I heard on the rest of the audio feed that night was the tick ticking of the wall clock, tick…tick…tick.

Back on the Quarter Deck in File 3 we recorded the team returning from our trip from the Main Hallway and A-Wing. We returned to the Quarter Deck to realize that the EMF spikes we had noticed earlier continued. We noted a .2, .3, .5, .6. We again tried to determine from where the spikes were emanating, taking reading off the overhead lights and the smoke detectors at ceiling height. Dave reported a .2. Again, we tried to determine where it might be coming from when Dave again registered a .2.

After returning from A-Wing as a group, the team decided to divide. Morrell and St. Michael's having supplied us with no sustainable evidence on the first investigation, we decided to divide our time between the Chapel and Drexel Hall only.

Dave and I departed for the Chapel, while Marie and Penny elected to remain in Drexel Hall. They had done a fairly lengthy session on C-Wing, and had returned to the Quarter Deck to take a break. They drank coffee on the Quarter Deck for a while before heading down to the basement.

It was during their coffee break, that Dave made a serious find in his evidence review that I had erroneously discounted the first time I had reviewed the findings. As the two ladies are taking a fairly lengthy coffee break on the Quarter Deck, the video recorder that was trained down C-Wing on the Main Hallway clearly picks up the sounds of walking. The footsteps appear to begin at D-Wing, walk down the Main Hallway behind the camera and stop at the Quarter Deck.

Now the reason I discounted the footsteps when first Dave presented them to me was that they were so life like that I assumed that they were caused by Dave walking. As I said earlier, he has a tendency to desire to be everywhere at once. At one point that night he had walked down to D-Wing, even though there are little to no accounts of activity on D-Wing.

Thus, when I heard the recording the first time, I just discounted it immediately. What I didn't understand, and wouldn't understand until rereviewing the evidence and the feeds was that Dave and I were actually doing a round in the Chapel at the time. Later in the recording the women actually make mention of that, as it was extremely hot that evening, and they wondered how we were making out in a stifling chapel.

What was also curious was that the women on the Quarter Deck would have said hello to Dave if he just suddenly walked up, but in the clip they continue to talk to each other, and never acknowledge anyone walking up to the Quarter Deck. The footsteps walk up to the Quarter Deck or the near vicinity of the Quarter Deck and just stop. There is a little scuffling noise as if a shoe had stopped moving…and then nothing.

Later, the women would settle in the gymnasium where all the teams had had odd occurrences on the first investigation.

The two women were vocalizing auditory experiences, hearing odd sounds in the gym. Then they decidedly hear unmistakable footsteps on the Quarter Deck, and Marie thought she heard the sound of a door opening. So distinct were the sounds of footsteps that they assumed Dave and I had returned from the Chapel. We had not, as they quickly surmised when we did not appear.

They also reported hearing footsteps to the back of the stage area where our guest investigators Gerard and Bob had also reported hearing such sounds on the first investigation. They didn't have audio evidence of the footsteps at the time, which led me to dismiss the claims. Now, however, I was hearing the same report. As I said before, layering evidence and claims on top of other evidence and claims is always interesting. If you have two groups claiming to have similar experiences, then my interest is heightened.

Penny was asking questions to Father Brown, the priest whose apparition had been seen by two different witnesses.

"Father Brown, did you teach them another language?" she asked, after which a distinct sound was captured that sounds like a footstep.

"Did you speak German?"

Marie apparently heard the footsteps because she said to Penny, "They're coming back."

Penny asks for clarification, "They're coming back?"

"I heard something. The door," Marie explained.

"The door?" asks Penny.

"I hear footsteps," confirmed Marie.

"Footsteps? You heard it?" Penny asks to confirm that Marie had also heard the footsteps.

"Ah ha," Marie said.

Marie greets whoever is making the sounds, "Hello."

Penny seconds the greeting, "Hello, hi, who is out there?"

"Yeah," Marie confirmed she was hearing footsteps.

"Yes!" remarked Penny. "Oh, I got the chills."

On the audio one can clearly hear the sounds of shuffling footsteps.

"Hello," Marie remarked.

"Hello, who are you?" asked Penny.

"My body is one big goose pimple," remarked Marie.

A couple more footsteps are heard to which Penny asked, "Did you hear that?"

"Oh, yeah," Marie responded.

Penny invited their unseen visitor, "Come on in."

"You can come closer to us," Marie offered.

"Come on in, we'd like to make your acquaintance. Speak in one of these recording devices. Tell us your name."

On the camera in the Quarter Deck, the sounds appear to cease. They must have moved into the gym because the two of them continue to affirm hearing the noises.

Penny decided to confirm what the two of them had been experiencing. "It is 8:40 pm and we have been hearing footsteps either out in the hallway or at the other end of the gym."

Marie must have been looking quizzically at the corner of the gym, because Penny pointedly asked, "Do you see something?"

"No, I hear something at the corner of the gym."

Dave and I would also do a turn in the gym during the night. Sitting on the stage, I asked, "Are you one of the Brothers?"

Directly afterwards, on the audio recorder was a response. It's a clear voice, apparently male. He mumbles what appears to be three words, but the message isn't decipherable.

Also, in the gymnasium that evening on Marie's audio recorder, which was sitting stationary on the stage, the team recorded a sound of something metal being moved. We were not in the gymnasium at the time. Obviously, the sound of something metal moving in an empty gym is curious.

Chapel

Robin and Dave in the Chapel

In the Chapel I used much the same set-up as the first time we investigated. I placed a quality video recorder in the Choir Loft approximately five feet above the floor, high enough not to be impeded by any animals that might be taking up residence. We did find small dung in the Choir Loft that looked to be squirrel droppings. Still, if a natural animal approached and moved the camera, the sound would have been picked up on the microphone, and it had not on the first investigation.

After having missed the moving of the rosary because the chandelier obstructed the view the first time around, I now moved the camera slightly off-center. Again, the camera was wired to an external battery pack that powered it for several hours. Having only caught the odd child's giggling in the basement of the Chapel, we also decided not to expend the hours of evidence review in the basement this time.

Almost from the moment I set up the camera in the Choir Loft, we started recording activity in the Chapel. I recorded in my log book that I got the camera set up and began recording. Almost immediately after, we recorded an EVP of a male voice saying, "I'm sorry," followed by an odd noise that sounded like a voice. To what he was referring I do not know.

Dave and I started our departure down the steps when 1.47 minutes into the recording we got a distinct male voice that said, "Hey," recorded on the camera, as if to say, "hey, where are you going?" After setup we departed the building, heading back to Drexel. After we left the building, at 2.27 minutes in on the recording I note that the camera is swaying, again seemingly to move on its own with absolutely no reason.

From having watched hours of still video in the Choir Loft as the sun went down slowly, I've noticed that the auto focus feature on the video camera will adjust itself to the shifts in lighting conditions. When this happens, there is an audible mechanical sound that the camera makes as it readjusts for the loss of light. Having figured out these automatic adjustments, I learned to discern between the auto focus adjustments and actual non-explained camera movements.

At 17.27 minutes in on the recording, I noted the same rubbing noises near the microphone again and slight camera movement as I noticed on the first investigation. I also noted in the log that I noticed the same movement "out of the corner of my eye" to the left of the Chapel that I had seen on the first investigation, that same aggravating, non-verifiable movement of something in motion within an empty space.

On the Chapel 4 file I note a big thumping sound in an empty building for which I could not account. At 13.02 minutes into the same file, I again recorded scratching sounds at the camera with slight camera movement. Again, what is moving a camera in an empty building, in an empty Choir Loft remains the question of the hour.

In the Chapel 5 file I recorded a weird sound at 6 minutes 27 seconds in. I do realize, as the light began to dim in the Chapel, that the auto focus is refocusing and the auto settings for iris and shutter speed are going to have to readjust. Night is falling. But at 8:35 minutes I noted a big camera movement. The light is definitely fading in this file and the auto focus is having to readjust.

In the Chapel 6 file, at 4:13 minutes in, there is another, unaccountable camera move that occurred, again in an empty building. At 18:19 minutes there is a sound near the camera that occurred and I wrote in my log book that the camera itself appeared to sway back and forth for several seconds. Again, this isn't the auto-focus adjusting for the loss of light, which makes a mechanical noise and appears to try to zoom in and out to readjust the focus.

At 20:56 minutes, Dave and I entered the building. I came up to the Choir Loft to try two IR illuminators that I had purchased. I quickly realized that the two illuminators were not up to the task of lighting an entire empty Chapel and removed them. At that time, we decided to leave the three ceiling chandeliers on, as there was no way to light the space adequately without them.

Interestingly, during the Chapel 7 file, I actually came in and adjusted the camera. While I'm adjusting the camera, there aren't any scratching sounds near the microphone, because I was making the adjustments to the shot from the actual tripod, versus moving the camera. As I reviewed the footage, I realized this was a good way to discern between actual human intervention with the camera and something that couldn't be explained as easily.

I'm a trained videographer. Hence, when I make adjustments to the camera, I do so at the tripod, and change the focal length with the zoom toggle. When I make adjustments to the camera, as I did that night, and which I notated in the log, it is a silent affair. I release the panning head, make the adjustment I need, and then tighten down the whole affair so the camera doesn't move from the position I'd put it in.

During the Chapel 7 file, Dave and I came back. I'd asked Dave to record some choir music at his church to play at the Chapel. Short sound bites often work best for this type of work, and he'd done a fantastic job of capturing some short segments to play in the Chapel to try to ignite some interest. Again, any time we can connect with energies, invigorate them to interact, the better. Dave played the short sound bites and we appeared to get some response on the EMF detector on the altar of a .2, then a 0.0. Then I recorded a low but detectable soft voice immediately afterwards. It wasn't an EVP that was of good enough quality to pursue. However, up in the Choir Loft, at 15:15 minutes, I notated a very large camera movement.

This is what I often refer to as layering. Any one of these taken on their own is little evidence that something paranormal is actually going on. However, if you play a piece of choir music and you get a short blip on an EMF detector, followed by a low, possible EVP, followed again by a camera movement in the Choir Loft, you get a much better feeling that something was actually being manipulated in the environment that evening that couldn't be accidental.

The camera movements took up much of the editing on the first investigation. By the second investigation, the camera movements were so prosaic that I didn't even bother entering them as video evidence. It's just part of the circus in the Chapel. Now, one might ask, as I certainly did, does the camera move on its own in other locations? It happened in this investigation at least once a file on average. I've had the same cameras for a number of years. I'll set them up and leave them recording for hours, and nothing has moved the camera.

That's not to say that as lighting conditions change the autofocus won't readjust. As I noted before, when the autofocus is adjusting to changing light conditions, there is a distinct mechanical sound in the camera and the camera will attempt to refocus, sometimes even zooming in or out slightly. These camera movements were different, distinctly different. It was as if something was trying to move the camera. Hence the scratching sound as if fingers were on the microphone.

I've only ever had camera movements like this at one other investigation. That was the camera set up in the master bedroom of the Octagon Mansion in Wytheville, Virginia, which honestly was another wild romp into the paranormal.

Dave and I were still in the Chapel during Chapel File 8. We came in and moved about the Chapel, trying to get something to respond with us. I recorded one quick spike of a 1.5 on the EMF recorder that I noted in the log. At 10:58 minutes on the video camera in the Choir Loft, I noted a long scratching sound at the mic and a camera move. Then at 13:19 seconds I jotted down on the log a weird noise that occurred right after Dave spoke. It was indistinct enough that I didn't pursue it further. At 13:41 minutes we readied ourselves to leave. Seven minutes later we caught a quiet, distant giggle, like a little girl amused that she'd evaded us.

During Chapel File 9, Penny and Marie came in to spend some time. They noted EMF spikes much higher than Dave and I had experienced. Penny calls them off as she receives them as 15.2, 4.8, and 4.2.

At 6:31 minutes in on Chapel File 9, I again logged camera movement in the Choir Loft. Penny and Marie depart the Chapel fairly quickly to take a walk outside. I do have to say that the night was stiflingly hot, and there is absolutely no air-conditioning in the building. So, while it was 98 degrees Fahrenheit outside, it was also 98 Fahrenheit in the building with absolutely no air movement.

While Dave and I stuck it out, Penny wasn't going to stay long in a building in which she was distinctly uncomfortable. Beautifully, at 9:10 minutes in on the feed, I noticed a hummingbird fly across the room. The small, magical bird had apparently made its home in the old Chapel, which leads me to wonder where it made its ingress and egress. Later, the two ladies come back into the building and the EMF again registered odd spikes of a .1, .2,

.3, .5, .6, .5, .3, .1, 4.4, .8 as if something were approaching the detector and then backing off.

Marie decided to take a sojourn up to the Choir Loft, despite the stifling heat, but Penny did not accompany her. At 13:44 minutes, as Marie ascended the stairs, I logged a camera move. At 14.20 minutes they reported a .1 on the EMF detector. As Marie was coming back down the stairs, at the camera there was a distinct EVP, a female voice this time saying, "There you go." Obviously, I love EVP's that indicate intelligence. It demonstrates that something in the space is witnessing the people in the environment and commenting on their comings and goings. In this case it knew that Marie was leaving the Choir Loft and made mention that she was leaving rather quickly. You do have to understand the heat of that late July evening. If the temperature on the ground was ninety-eight degrees, the Choir Loft was probably closer to 100.

During Chapel File 10 there was no living person in the building and thus absolutely no one engaged with the equipment. Yet still, the machinations continued. At 2:08 I logged a camera movement in the Choir Loft. Again, at 20:20 minutes I recorded a long scratching sound and camera movement. I distinctly wrote that the camera doesn't move so much as it jumps up and down, "as if something had bumped into the camera."

Again, during the Chapel 11 video file the building again was completely empty. Still, 15 minutes, 15 seconds into the recording, I noticed a scratching sound at the mic on the video recorder in the Choir Loft and a slight camera move.

The Chapel 12 video file continued to deliver activity. At 20:34 minutes, as I recorded in the log book, I noted sounds and a slight whisper. Then at 21:20 seconds, I noticed the sound of something being moved. Nothing was recorded on the camera moving, but the sound was distinct.

In the Chapel 13 file feed it was noted that there was an odd sound like a light bulb popping. At 5:19 there was a knocking sound for which I could not account. Again, at 5:40 and 6:42, there were odd sounds I couldn't identify. In the log book I wrote down my notes, but also highlighted the documentation meaning that I was intrigued by the sounds and intended to go back and investigate further. However, the sheer plethora of activity in the two buildings that night meant that I couldn't possibly rereview every odd sound because the team would never get through all of the evidence if we did. Some investigations, though not many, leave that much trace behind them.

During the Chapel 13 feed the entire team came out to the building. We arrived at 15:35. At 16:09 the sounds of the Chapel door being opened, the same sounds that I had heard during the Chapel 11 file, repeated. The team entered and immediately started noticing EMF spikes of a .2, .1. Not exactly exciting, but still unaccounted.

Seventeen minutes in I decided to ascend the stairs to the Choir Loft, probably wanting to check the battery level on the video camera. I do record that I adjusted the camera slightly… with no camera noise evident. Then I came back downstairs. At 19:19 Penny started registering spikes on her EMF detector of a 4.8, 1.9. At 21:43 she reported a 2.5. At 22:11 the team reported a quick succession of EMF spikes, 1.7, 1.3, 1.0, .7, .8, .1, 11.0.

At 22.20 the spikes continued to be recorded verbally at a 1.7, 1.9, 2.5, .6, .8, 1.6, 1.7, .8, .2.

The team left the building not too long afterwards. No sooner did we depart the building then I recorded a camera move and scratching sounds at the microphone.

During Video file 14 Dave and I returned to the building. Dave and I had a close connection with the building that Penny and Marie perhaps did not feel. I'd fallen in love with the Chapel during those long-ago years when I'd first glimpsed it from the road. Dave had actually had the opportunity to perform in the building once for a Christmas concert a few years previously. During our first investigation, the Christmas decorations from that previous choir concert were still hanging on the pillars of the old church. They'd been removed before our second investigation.

Dave and I came to the door at three minutes, forty-four seconds into the recording. I noted the door opening in my log. At 4:02, I also note a lot of whispering. It's likely Dave, because it was a high-pitched male voice, and Dave was definitely reacting to the extreme heat of the evening.

We decided to utilize the bible that was on the altar to do some bible readings, again to see if we could elicit something to give us a response. I chose the first reading, but lacking my reading glasses it was a halting performance. Still, I fell in love with the poetic elements of the verse that have never left me. Perhaps the Catholic priests were there that evening breathing in my ear with the beauty of Isaiah 32:15 and the Liturgy of the Hours:

> "In the old days, the spirits of the hours....
> Then will the desert become an orchard.
> Then will the orchard become regarded as a forest.
> Right will dwell in the desert, and justice reside in the orchard.
> Justice will bring about peace.
> Right will bring along calm.
> My people will live in a peaceful country. In quiet restful places.
> My people will live in quiet places."

Dave said that he could visually see the chandeliers dimming and flaring while I read. Upon reviewing the video, I didn't see any discernible differences in the lights. However, on the EMF detector on the altar I did note some quick spikes.

Dave continued with some bible passage readings. I'm not sure what they were; they didn't strike me as quite that eloquent, nor as perfect to the setting, as the one I had stumbled upon. Nothing God can do to smite the sinners and redeem the forgiven will ever detract from the promise of living in those silent, peaceful spaces.

After he finished the bible reading, however, from the Choir Loft, the video recorder recorded a Class A EVP that responded, "It is credible," in response. It seemed to agree that we had done justice to the bible that evening. The voice in the recording was definitely male and rather distinct. It is obvious that it isn't Dave, who I believe was talking at the time down near the altar. Dave too has a very distinct voice that makes it very easy to discern what is and isn't Dave speaking.

The quality of the recording is excellent, and there is absolutely no mistaking what it is saying, as is the case with so many EVP's, hence one person will hear one word, someone will decipher something completely different. What is really interesting about this EVP is that it somehow hides itself in the ambient sound of the room. Hence when I play it for people, they will miss it the first time, and wonder what I'm getting at. It's usually on the second hearing that they finally hear it. Then I watch as their face registers amazement, and they wonder why something so plainly there could be missed.

There also appeared to be some whispering going on in the background before the EVP is captured, as if someone or someone's were discussing something to which our unseen male confirmed that the readings were, "credible."

I hoped our male speaker was enjoying living in that old Chapel which is definitely peaceful and quiet, where hummingbirds flew and the dust motes were illuminated by the light of century old stained-glass windows as time ticked slowly by.

At 10:58, again in the Choir Loft, the camera moved again. And as we prepared to leave the Chapel that evening, again we got a very distant EVP of a child giggling in the distance...perhaps from the basement. The Chapel is never completely silent it seems, even when it is "quiet."

As the camera was starting Video File 15, Dave and I were getting ready to head back to Drexel. Fifteen minutes later I note a large popping sound, almost like a lightbulb bursting in the empty Chapel. It wasn't the light bulbs, however, as the camera had the three chandeliers in its view. At 16:30 I also noted a slight camera movement, this time without the rubbing noises at the microphone.

During Video File 16, at 12:04, I recorded another camera movement, this one fairly long in duration. During the evidence review for the second investigation I discounted the camera movements in our findings. It just happened with such regularity that I feared that my credibility might be brought into question. However, I've worked with these cameras for years, both shooting side jobs, and at my place of employment where I created training videos. Aside from the auto focus adjusting itself in different lighting situations, they don't move on their own. If it had been an animal, I would also have heard the sounds of movement on the wood floor, and it was silent up in the Choir Loft. Something unseen appeared to be fascinated with the camera equipment.

Then at 20:02 I heard the door to the Chapel squeak, as if someone was coming in. It was so clearly the door that I waited, perplexed, for the sounds of a team coming in. But no one did come in, which left me confused. Could it have been a breeze blowing the door slightly open? It's possible, but it's the only time that I'd heard the sound of the door moving in either investigation. And the night was still, sticky and hot. Still, if there's a whisper of doubt, we don't present it to our clients. It became another bit of an oddity that I left behind.

At 7:41 in Video file 17 I noticed another camera movement with an odd clicking sound afterward.

During Chapel File 18 I noticed sounds near the camera in the Choir Loft. Then at 3:15 the same rubbing sounds at the camera. During Chapel File 19 at 3:39 again the rubbing sound was heard at the camera and then camera movement was detected. The same occurred at 17:28.

Video file 20 was quiet with only the sounds of the bugs buzzing and bumping against the windows, or burning themselves on the light bulbs that illuminated the empty building all night.

During Chapel File 21, the last of the night, I noted the final camera movement at 5:16 which I described as more of a jerking motion. We came in at 12:22 and started breaking down the equipment after a long, long night.

The audio recorder on the altar was mainly quiet that evening, as it had been on the first investigation. Perhaps the spirits respect the sanctity of the altar itself. Noted were some sounds in the Chapel three times that sounded like footsteps in an empty building.

Back at Drexel Hall

Throughout the night the Main Hallway and Quarter Deck continued to be quite active.

Rather early in the evening, Dave and I headed out to the Chapel for the first time. Marie and Penny decided to take another turn in A-Wing. They departed down the main hallway. On the recording I could hear them talking while they walked away. Then I also detected the sound of a higher pitched voice humming two notes. I wrote excitedly in my log, "12:50 singing!" I immediately scratched it out thinking the humming was probably Marie or Penny, and thought nothing about it afterwards. It's the beauty of writing and rereviewing the evidence where you make new discoveries in the material.

When Marie and Penny returned from A-Wing, they stopped to get a cup of coffee on the Quarter Deck as I explained earlier. They were talking as they poured their libations, and discussed the fact that while on A-Wing they thought they'd heard the sound of singing. I hadn't until this moment realized that the entry I had crossed out had been the same singing that they were now discussing, and they had heard it with their own ears. Sometimes, pieces in the puzzle get lost under the sheer volume of material left to review. Again, we had captured the sounds of singing in an otherwise empty building, and we just didn't know it. However, this recording was by no means as clear and remarkable as on our first investigation. Still, it was clearly humming in a building known for the sounds of singing.

They were also registering EMF spikes again on the Quarter Deck of a .1, .2, .7, .5, .3, .2. As I was listening back over the Hallway 8 video feed, I also made another discovery, a short EVP that sounded like a male voice talking over the top of Marie and

Penny as they discussed how hot it was in the Chapel. It's quick and indiscernible as to what is being said, but it's definitely there and definitely neither of them.

As I said, the sheer volume of material meant that no matter how careful we were, something would get missed. The sheer volume of weird happenings means things moving in empty rooms and voices breaking out in song clearly keep the party rolling as long as the recorders record, and the listeners are careful in the review.

Dave and I were taking a turn in the gymnasium, and Marie and Penny were on the Quarter Deck during the Main Hall 9 Video File. Two minutes in they were again registering spikes on the meter of a 1.4, 1.7, 1.2 and then a 0. It's 9:00 p.m. when they decided to head toward A-Wing on the Main Hall. Marie remarked about a crazy leap on her detector of a 5.1 and then reported feeling goose bumps while the spikes continued .3, .5, .7, .1, .7. As they're walking, I continue to hear Penny name off the EMF spikes she was detecting until I can no longer hear the sound of their voices and the Quarter Deck and Main Hall are completely silent. At 6:57 on the recording I noted a quiet sound like a distant exhale and then the quiet continued. Thirteen minutes later they returned and Penny exclaims she had a 22.4 spike on the meter followed by a 6.9. A couple of minor spikes followed.

They decided to take a walk outside. You hear them depart out of the doors and the file ends.

Whistling on the Quarter Deck

On the video recorders that evening we also recorded some very distinct whistling. At 11:11 p.m., as Penny and Marie were departing out to investigate the Chapel, there is the distinct noise of the double doors being opened by them and then a whistling sound as if to indicate, "there they go."

Later, when we were all in the building and on the Quarter Deck, Dave brought along an electronic cat ball. The electronic cat ball is something new we were trying out. It makes no sound and shows no lights unless it is moved. Marie was demonstrating how to move the cat ball to make the lights turn on, trying to get something interested in moving the cat ball. Marie asks quite pointedly, "Now, can you do that? Your turn."

Immediately, the video again recorded a whistling sound as if something was interacting.

C-Wing

C-Wing that evening didn't fail in providing the team interesting evidence, as it had on the first investigation. Yet, it continued to seem that C-Wing preferred to produce evidence when the investigators were not present.

Earlier in the evening, after set-up, we also recorded an EVP that seems to be female. Again, no one was in C-Wing, though the team can be heard on the Quarter Deck. The female voice appears to be saying, "I want, what I want, when I want it." Perhaps our floating nun was making her desires known? Again, it's clearly a female voice that is not one of us. And again, there is no mistaking what the female is saying, clearly a Class A EVP.

A couple hours into the investigation, Marie and Penny were taking their aforementioned coffee break on the Quarter Deck, with Dave and I in the Chapel. This was then the remarkable footsteps are caught walking in the Main Hallway seeming to start near D-Wing, move behind the camera on C-Wing and stop at or near the Quarter Deck. The same footsteps that the women never indicated they heard.

The school was on summer break at the time; thus, we had the buildings completely to ourselves. No night time custodians or cleaning staff would be in the building on a Saturday night in the middle of July. Indeed, we saw no other people on the property that night at all. And if a person had approached the Quarter Deck, the women would have responded in some manner. I also realized that the footsteps walk up to the Quarter Deck, stop, and then are never heard again.

Two video files later, you hear the sound of the door opening and closing as Marie and Penny depart the building. There are no other sounds evident except the AC unit humming in an empty C-Wing. Then two little footsteps are heard, and then stop, a minute later another clandestine footstep as if someone were sneaking around, trying very hard not to be heard. These footsteps were not as distinct as the ones earlier, which were undeniably footsteps I had falsely assumed were Dave's. Again, the sounds of footsteps are often reported.

The team caught a remarkable EVP fairly early in the night on the video camera set up to record down C-Wing. The team was on the Quarter Deck at the time, and you can hear us speaking. One can hear each of us speaking softly when a very low bass male voice is recorded on the audio of the video camera. The voice is undeniable. It is there, it is irrefutable, but what message it is trying to convey is not quite clear. Upon reviewing it for the writing of this book, it sounded like "selling shirts." While I realize that may make no sense whatsoever, this was the closest I could come to in deciphering the words.

What is undeniable is the fact that the voice was a very low, very bass voice. Dave, our one male investigator that evening, has an unusually high voice. As in the Chapel, it is undeniable that the voice we hear on the recording is not, could not possibly be Dave's voice.

It was around 9:00 p.m. that evening, and the teams had dispersed to other parts of the building. The Quarter Deck is completely quiet. On C-wing there is the sound of a door handle being moved and a door opened. It is quite obviously not the main entrance door, but sounds more like the door to a classroom. Roughly three minutes later, the recorder picks up the sound of a door quietly closing. Again, there was no one in the vicinity. This phenomena has been reported to me as happening numerous times. As the door does not appear to open and close in the hall, the sound must have come from behind the camera, which makes me wonder if it isn't the sound of the basement door.

Late in the night on C-Wing, a rempod which we had placed in the middle of the hall seemingly went berserk. This went on for several minutes as the rempod sent out a few shrill notes and then ramped up to a succession of longer small notes and finally a continuous cacophony before falling abruptly silent. As all this is dying out, fascinatingly, there is clearly again the sound of a door closing. Again, the camera detects no doors moving, meaning that the door must have been behind the camera, or it is a residual sound. The team was not in the area nor did anyone hear the noises.

Two investigations, countless hours of video and audio feeds, hours of interviews and historical research. Three years later, after walking into First State Military Academy on that Saturday afternoon, I had no idea how far this journey would take me. I've often quipped to Marie that First State is Delaware's Skin Walker Ranch. But that's not quite accurate, as the souls that appear trapped or recorded into the fabric of First State are not at all negative; they're just there. Einstein first suggested that time isn't linear as we perceive it, that it ebbs and flows back on itself in ways that our material presence cannot fathom. Perhaps the beings that inhabit First State aren't actually ghosts at all. They're just beings that inhabit the space in their own time, as we inhabit it now in ours. Ballroom dancers dancing a waltz, an out of time janitor vacuuming the floor in a dorm room without electricity, a boy running up to the building and then disappearing, a priest with a bible walking Morrell Hall, so life-like that the construction workers perceive him as real. First State…Providence Creek Academy…St. Joseph's Industrial School is a living time capsule that plays itself out on a daily basis to anyone interested in listening. As an investigator, I am privileged to have played a part.

Thank you to the following people for making this book be possible:

I would like to thank Janet for having the trust in us to call the team in to begin with. Thank you for the tour of the basement of the Chapel and the Chapel itself. If you ever want to become an investigator, you're more than welcome to come on board.

I would also like to thank Patrick Gallucci for allowing a team in at all. We were the interlopers and I never lose sight of that. As a leader of an educational institution, it meant a lot to us that you would trust us with your secrets and give us free reign of the buildings.

Audrey Erschen, thank you for sharing your experiences. The two dancers doing a waltz was mind blowing. Though PCA no longer inhabits the buildings, still your experiences had a great deal of influence developing these pages.

Chuck Taylor, thank you as well for sharing the information. The boy that disappeared has perplexed for a long time now. Would that we could come up with a reasonable explanation.

Dave Sadler, always the dependable one. Thank you for your service and hard work, and also for the free coffee (which we always need) and the food (which we *always* appreciate).

Marie Williamson, the woman who can ride or drive anything, I depend on you more than just to parallel park my car, though I can't do that either. Marie lends a scientific perspective so often missing in paranormal investigators. She was the one that informed us of the sun flares occurring on the night of the team's second investigation. I couldn't do what I do without a mind like yours.

Collin Wintjen is my oldest paranormal investigator colleague. Though he lives on the West Coast, he can always be called upon for evidence review. Thank you for all the hours of work that I would otherwise have done myself.

Thank you to my editor, Trent Scott, whose sage advice was very much appreciated, despite the meagre wages offered. Thank you for your time and effort in making the publication of the book possible.

Some of the names in this book were changed to protect the identity of the individual. Either the team did not have permission to use their names, or the people described could not be contacted.

I apologize for any mistakes or mis-interpretation of the facts as presented. I did extensive research and interviewing during the process of writing the book. However, mistakes may still be made.

Resources

Aikens, Thomas (December 5, 2021) Recorded phone interview.

Barbara (last name unknown). (November 24, 2010). "St. Joseph's Industrial School for Colored Boys." My Colorful Life. Retrieved July 7. 2024 from My Colorful Life: St. Joseph's Industrial School for Colored Boys (barbinde.blogspot.com)

Cressy, Leah (October 17, 2020) Recorded phone interview.

Dobrijevic, Daisy (July 6, 2022). "Solar Flares: What are they and how do they affect Earth." Space.com. Retrieved April 28, 2024.

Erschen, Audrey (February 14, 2022) Recorded phone interview.

Forrest, Janet (July 2021) Recorded video interview and walk through, various correspondences.

Gallucci, Patrick (February, 14, 2022) Recorded phone interview.

"Great Migration; African American History." (2023). Editors of Encyclopedia Britannic Great Migration| Definition, History, & Facts | Britannica. Retrieved February 25, 2023.

Hatton, Leon (February 14, 2022) Recorded phone interview.

Harvey, Scott (2022) Recorded phone interview.

Horton, William. (December 5, 2021) Recorded phone interview.

Johnson, Dr. Yasmith (2022) Recorded phone interview.

"Locust Grove House Home of Governor Joshua Clayton. (Anonymous). Delaware Public Archives. Retrieved July 7, 2024 from, Locust Grove House Home of Governor Joshua Clayton - Delaware Public Archives - State of Delaware.

"Powerful solar flare to disrupt communications" Kirland Media Posted July 17, 2023 on YouTube. Retrieved April 28, 2024.

Skay, Leah (December 12, 2021) Recorded Phone Interview.

"St. Katharine Drexel" Encyclopedia Britannica Saint Katharine Drexel | Biography, Facts, & Miracles | Britannica Retrieved February 5, 2023.

"St. Katherine Drexel's Story." Anonymous. Saint Katharine Drexel | Franciscan Media Retrieved February 19, 2023.

"St. Katharine Drexel." Philanthropy Roundtable. St. Katharine Drexel - Philanthropy Roundtable Retrieved February 19, 2023.

Sobel, Robert, and John Raimo, eds. Biographical Directory of the Governors of the United States, 1789-1978, Vol. 1, Westport, Conn.; Meckler Books, 1978. 4 vols. Retrieved July 7, 2024 from Joshua Clayton - National Governors Association (nga.org)

"St. Polycarp Parish History." 1918 to Present" (Anonymous) Parish History – Saint Polycarp Church. Retrieved February 25, 2023.

"Sunspots and Solar Flares" (Anonymous) Nasa Science Space Place. Updated July 22, 2021. Retrieved April 28, 2024.

Taylor, Chuck. "History of St. Joesphs Industrial School." [PowerPoint Presentation] provided by former PCA St. Joseph's Foundation Founding Board Member on March 10, 2022.

Taylor, Chuck. Managing Director, Head of School Providence Creek Academy. (April 2, 2022) Recorded phone interview.

Tingley, Brett. (July 22, 2022). "Sun Outburst prompts warnings of moderate solar storm this weekend. Space.com. Retrieved April 28, 2022.

"Who Was Francis A. Drexel?" Who Was Francis A. Drexel? – Saint Joseph's University Libraries (sju.edu) Retrieved February, 5 2023.

www.ingramcontent.com/pod-product-compliance
Lightning Source LLC
Chambersburg PA
CBHW071203160426
43196CB00011B/2183